HISTORY OF
THE DIOCESE OF HARRISBURG

PROTESTANT EPISCOPAL CHURCH

1904 – 1954

By

RALPH T. WOLFGANG
Rector of the Church of the Holy Trinity
Hollidaysburg, Pa.

with foreword
By

THE RT. REV. JOHN THOMAS HIESTAND, D. D., S. T. D.
Bishop of Harrisburg

Published by the Diocese of Harrisburg
1954

Printed by the SELINSGROVE TIMES-TRIBUNE
MAY, 1954

ST. STEPHEN'S CATHEDRAL
Harrisburg

FOREWARD

It is a privilege indeed to write a foreword to this short History of the Diocese of Harrisburg.

The purpose of all histories is to preserve for the generations of the future, something of the events and the lives of the men and women who largely shaped these events that we might know of the faith and the struggles that gave us our heritage which we strive to preserve and enlarge for those who shall come after us.

This the writer of this history has accomplished with a clarity of thought and expression which speaks for itself.

It was my privilege to know many of the Clergy and laity who gave so much of themselves to the work of the Church during the fifty years in which the Diocese has grown in numbers and influence here in Central Pennsylvania.

As we read the following pages, it becomes increasingly clear, that had the resources of these faithful and devoted servants of God and His Church, matched their faith and enthusiasm, the Episcopal Church in the Diocese of Harrisburg would be considerably larger and more effective in this our day.

As one who shares in this inheritance, may I express the hope that we who read this history, give increasingly of our loyalty, our devotion and our means, that the good work, begun by God, may be brought to still greater achievement.

In concluding this foreword, I would express my personal appreciation and the appreciation of our Diocesan Family, to the Rev. Ralph T. Wolfgang for his untiring work in making this history possible.

JOHN THOMAS HEISTAND,
Bishop of Harrisburg.

Harrisburg, April 8, 1954.

TABLE OF CONTENTS

ILLUSTRATIONS

THE EPISCOPAL CHURCH IN THE DIOCESE OF HARRISBURG

Chapter One

THE FORMATION OF THE DIOCESE

I

On Tuesday evening, November 29, 1904, forty-nine clergymen and ninety-one laymen assembled in St. James Church in Lancaster. They had gathered to set in motion the machinery for the functioning of a new Diocese which had been created by a division of the Diocese of Central Pennsylvania. Seated in a church whose architecture was a visible reminder that its history stretched back 160 years to a time when Lancaster was a frontier town in colonial Pennsylvania, these delegates must have been aware of the great cloud of witnesses who watched to see whether the faith of the fathers was evident in the children of the twentieth century. Thus it was a solemn task on which they were engaged. The parishes which these men represented had fought an eight-year fight for the privilege of standing alone. Could these men so plan, under the guidance of the Holy Spirit, that the new Diocese would set forth the cause of Christ and His Church?

Some of the older delegates could remember that the question of the division of the Diocese of Central Pennsylvania had first arisen twenty-five years before when Dr. Charles Breck, Dean of the Convocation of Williamsport, presented a memorial to the Convention of 1879 urging that his Convocation be set apart as a new Diocese. This proposal, if adopted, would have created a small Diocese consisting of the counties of Lycoming, Clinton, Centre, Tioga, Potter, Northumberland, Montour, Columbia, Union and Snyder—essentially the northwestern portion of our present Diocese. Opposition was immediate, and came from within the Convocation. Under the leadership of the Reverend Louis Zahner, Rector of St. Paul's, Bloomsburg, a resolution of protest was introduced. The friends of division were strong enough to bring Dr. Breck's resolution to a vote with the result that the clergy supported it by a comfortable margin, while the laity, by a slightly narrower margin, voted it down. Since the consent of both orders was necessary to proceed with division, nothing could be done.

(1)

While division was killed on the convention floor, it was by no means a dead issue. Dr. Breck reintroduced his resolution at the Convention of 1880. Two counter proposals were submitted, each altering somewhat the boundaries of the proposed Diocese. After sharp debate, a committee of six was appointed to study the question of division and report to the next convention. This committee reported to the Convention of 1881 that it considered a division of the Diocese unwise. Undaunted by this opposition, Dr. Breck succeeded in having the whole question of Episcopal relief referred to a committee of sixteen which was to study the question and report to the Convention of 1882. In order to have something definite on which to base their deliberations, the committee submitted the following questionnaire to the clergy and vestries of the organized parishes:

1. In your opinion, is more Episcopal oversight needed for interests of the Church in your vicinity?
2. If there is such a need, how do you think it should be supplied?
3. If you think a division of the Diocese is necessary, on what lines should the division be made?
4. In case of division, how much would you agree to raise toward the endowment fund of the Diocese in which your parish would be situated?

The returns from this questionnaire showed that about 35% of the Diocese believed that more Episcopal oversight was needed; the Diocese was about equally divided on division and the election of an assistant Bishop; only 11% favored division on the lines of the Williamsport Convocation; finally, there seemed to be no disposition on the part of the Diocese to increase the endowment fund or to pay increased assessments. In view of these facts, the committee felt justified in reporting against any division of the Diocese. This committee had been instructed to confer with the Bishop regarding his wish for an Assistant Bishop. Bishop Howe told the committee that he would welcome such an election, and, with this report, the convention of 1882 gave no consideration to division. It was not till the Convention of 1884, however, that the Diocese succeeded in electing an Assistant Bishop. The election and consecration of the Reverend Nelson S. Rulison brought to an end the first chapter in the struggle for the division of the Diocese of Central Pennsylvania.

The question of division may have been taken from the convention floor, but during the next dozen years it was a matter of informal discussion by interested clergy and laity. The discussion became less academic in 1895 when Bishop Rulison became the Diocesan and the question of Episcopal relief once more seemed pertinent. So insistent did the discussion become that Bishop Rulison felt impelled to comment upon it in his address to the Convention of 1896:

"There are many among us who think division desirable, but I have not found among either clergy or laity a general and spontaneous sense of need and demand for a division. My own judgment is that we shall be compelled at no remote time to face the question; and I am desirous and willing that preparations shall be made for it. But I am anxious that when the time shall come the question may be settled on sound principles and in the right way. There is a dignity and an influence that are always associated with strength and never with weakness, and because of this most Churchmen prefer to belong to a strong Diocese rather than a weak one. If a division of our own Diocese would reduce its size without diminishing its strength, all of us, I suppose, would favor it. But we know that would be impossible. Any division of our territory would at once greatly diminish the relative importance of our Diocese in the General Church, and make two comparatively weak Dioceses where there is now one strong one. But if that result to us would prove of great advantage to the Kingdom of God, I, at least, should offer no objection to it. The best interests of the Church at large are more important than Diocesan pride or power. We should decide first of all whether these interests demand a division or not."

The attitude of the Bishop put an end to the hopes of those who sought an early division of the Diocese, but the situation suddenly changed with his death a year later. The committee which was appointed to inform the Right Reverend Ethelbert Talbot of his election as Bishop of the Diocese told him of the sentiment for division, and they were given the impression that the new Bishop would not oppose such a project. Any doubt of the Bishop's attitude was removed when in the address to his first Convention which met in June, 1898, he stated that he favored a division of the Diocese at the earliest possible moment. He made it clear that the consent of General Convention could not be asked until a proper dividing line could be agreed upon and until the sum of $100,000 could be raised to provide an endowment fund of $50,000 for the support of the Bishop in each of the proposed Dioceses. Acting on this suggestion, Convention appointed a committee which recommended that immediate steps be taken to follow the Bishop's recommendation and they hopefully asserted that the division could be accomplished in three years.

It was one thing to adopt a program with enthusiasm in Convention, but quite another to take it to the parishes and work it out in detail. It was one thing to agree to division, quite another to establish a boundary line with which all would be satisfied. The committee appointed to recommend a demarcation line between the two Dioceses reported to the Convention of 1899 only to have their line rejected. Another committee suggested to the Convention in 1900 six possible ways by which the Diocese might be divided without any particular recommendation. The result was that Convention adopted the line it had rejected the year before. According to this action, a Northern and a Southern Diocese would be created. The Northern Diocese would have embraced the Archdeaconries of Scranton and Williamsport including such centers as Carbondale, Scranton, Wilkes-Barre, Bloomsburg, Sunbury, Williamsport, Lock Haven and Bellefonte. The Archdeaconries of Reading and Harrisburg would be combined into the Southern Diocese with such centers as Easton, Bethlehem, Allentown, Reading, Lebanon, Lancaster, York, Carlisle, Harrisburg and Altoona.

The talk of raising the endowment fund proved even more difficult. Before people would open their pocketbooks, they wanted to know the nature of the Diocese to which they would belong. The line of division adopted in 1900 did not prove popular and the committee reported that it had been unable to raise the desired amount, so the Convention of 1901 rescinded the action of the year before and the whole matter reverted to the status of 1898. The impasse might have continuel indefinitely had not Bishop Talbot brought the matter to a head in 1903. He stated to the Convention that some sort of Episcopal relief was absolutely necessary and that he would consent either to division or to the election of a Coadjutor. The committee to act on the Bishop's request made two reports—the majority favored division and the minority recommended the election of a Coadjutor. The majority report was adopted and a new committee was appointed to try to raise the necessary endowment with the understanding that the sum raised would be credited to the contributing parishes.

In preparing for division the impression was that it would follow the line of 1900. The Convention of 1904 must have been surprised, therefore, when the Bishop stated in his address that

"all divisions hitherto effected in the American Church have had in view one strong, compact parent Diocese, able to meet the obligations and maintain the rate of expenditure already assumed; and another Diocese with resources such as we know will justify the belief that it will be self-supporting."

On this basis he recommended that the parent Diocese consist of the Archdeaconries of Scranton and Reading, and the new Diocese, the Archdeaconries of Harrisburg and Williamsport. In support of this recommendation, he pointed out that the parent Diocese would have an endowment of $47,296.35 while the endowment of the new Diocese would be $22,502; the parent Diocese would contain 75 parishes with 55 in the new; the parent Diocese would be served by 71 clergymen while 55 would be at work in the new; the parent Diocese would have a communicant strength of 11,031 while the communicant strength in the new Diocese would be 7,887. He pointed out that the railroads, rivers and mountains so unite the various sections that it would be possible for the Bishops to reach the furthest limit of their Dioceses in a few hours, and that this was the only line which could secure a community of interest both socially and economically. Moreover, he clinched his point by stating that this was the only line of division to which he would give his consent.

Fortunately, the canons of the Church did not stipulate what amount a new Diocese need have in hand for the support of the Episcopate. The goal of $150,000 which the Diocese had set for itself in 1902 had not been achieved. The committee reported to the Convention of 1904 that it had been able to raise only $43,292.81. Since the line of division recommended by the Bishop met all the canonical requirements, Convention took the necessary steps to divide the Diocese. General Convention gave its consent that fall and, on October 12, the Bishop issued the call for the Primary Convention in the new Diocese.

It must have been with mixed emotions that the 140 delegates to this Primary Convention made their journey to Lancaster. Some would have preferred the election of a Coadjutor to division; others would have preferred division along the lines of 1900; some had misgivings about the increased financial burdens the establishment of a new Diocese would entail; others were fired with enthusiasm at the prospect of real advance for the Church in Central Pennsylvania. So, with mingled hopes and fears they waited quietly in their places and breathed their silent prayers while they waited for the Reverend Robert S. Nichols, Rector of St. Paul's Church, Bloomsburg, to begin the reading of the service and Evening Prayer.

II

While launching a new Diocese is unquestionably a pioneering enterprise the men gathered at Lancaster were not without experience. They knew the law of the Church and the steps which they must take; church politics had become familiar through participation in the conventions of the Diocese of Central Pennsylvania and through serving on its committees; and they knew each other's strengths and weaknesses. So, when Bishop Talbot called the Convention to order after the Evening Prayer, they were not at a loss to attend to the business at hand.

After the formality of reading the call for the Convention, the acting Secretary, Mr. Charles M. Clement of Sunbury, was unanimously elected Secretary of the Diocese. The Bishop then officially announced his intention of remaining with the "old" Diocese and thereupon vacated the chair. The Convention then completed its organization by electing the following officers: President, Rev. LeRoy F. Baker, the senior priest and Rector of St. Paul's Church, Harrisburg; Treasurer, William K. Aldicks of Harrisburg; and Chancellor, John G. Freeze of Bloomsburg. After offering to Bishop Talbot a resolution of appreciation, Convention placed the Diocese under his care till such time as a Bishop could be elected and consecrated.

(6)

After considerable debate, the salary of the Bishop was fixed at $4,000 a year together with the free use of an Episcopal residence which was to be rented by the Standing Committee at an amount not to exceed $500. Considering the value of the dollar in 1904, it will be seen that the present salary of the Bishop ($9,000) is not a great advance.

The first real problem of the Diocese was to choose a name. Three Names were submitted: "Diocese of Harrisburg," "Diocese of the Susquehanna," and "Diocese of Williamsport." On the first ballot, someone wrote in "Diocese of Lancaster." By the process of elimination, "Diocese of Harrisburg" was selected on the third ballot.

The rest of the evening was spent presenting nominations to fill the various offices except that of Bishop.

Wednesday's session began at 9:00 with a service of Holy Communion celebrated by the Bishop and the two Lancaster clergy. During the morning session, the balloting for the several offices was interspersed with the transaction of routine business. It was not until that afternoon that the results of the election were known. Since it is of interest to the modern reader to know the names of those who were to take leadership in the Diocese, we give here the results of the election.

Registrar: Rev. Robert F. Gibson (Steelton).

Standing Committee: The Rev. Messrs. Charles Morrison (Sunbury), President; William F. Shero (Lancaster), Secretary; LeRoy F. Baker (Harrisburg); Walter R. Breed (Lancaster); George I. Brown (Bellefonte); and the Messrs. Levi B. Alricks (Harrisburg); Ivanhoe S. Huber (Shamokin); H. B. Meredith (Danville); Benjamin F. Meyers (Harrisburg); and Hugh M. North (Columbia).

Finance Committee: (ex officio Trustees of the Endowment Fund) Messrs. Charles M. Clement (Sunbury); William K. Alricks (Harrisburg); John F. Freeze (Bloomsburg); James M. Lamberton (Harrisburg); Allen P. Pearley (Williamsport); Samuel H. Reynolds (Lancaster);; and George S. Schmidt (York).

Department of Missions

The Venerable LeRoy F. Baker, Archdeacon of Harrisburg; the Venerable William Heakes, Archdeacon of Williamsport and Rector of St. Paul's Church, Wellsboro; Rev. Edward H. Eckel, Christ Church, Williamsport; Rev. Franklin T. Eastment, Lewistown, and the Messrs. W. Fred Reynolds (Bellefonte); George N. Reynolds (Lancaster); William K. Alricks (Harrisburg); Grier Hersh (York); Frank G. Angle (Danville); and W. A. Robinson (Coudersport).

When all other business had been disposed of, the Convention reached its climax in the nomination and election of a Bishop. Local talent was not wanting in aspiring to fill this important post. Complimentary nominations were given Rev. Charles Morrison of Sunbury, Rev. LeRoy F. Baker of Harrisburg, and Rev. Alexander McMillan of Carlisle. These gentlemen recognized the nature of these nominations by promptly withdrawing their names. The serious contenders from within the Diocese were: Rev. Charles J. Wood of York, Rev. Walter R. Breed of St. James, Lancaster, Rev. Edward H. Eckel of Christ Church, Williamsport, and Rev. George C. Foley of Trinity Church, Williamsport. From outside the Diocese the following were named: The Rt. Rev. Peter T. Rowe, Missionary Bishop of Alaska; Rev. Charles F. J. Wrigley, Rev. Alexander Mann, Rev. William T. Manning, Rev. Robert Talbot, Rev. Frank DuMoulin, Rev. Edgar Cope, and Rev. Charles Scadding. The high calibre of these non-Diocesan men may be gauged by the fact that at least four of them subsequently became Bishops of the Church.

When the voting began the Rev. Edward H. Eckel and the Rev. George C. Foley led on the first three ballots. On the fourth ballot, the laity showed a decided trend to Rev. William T. Manning and, after nine ballots, Dr. Manning received a majority of the votes in both orders and was declared elected. On motion of Rev. Franklin T. Eastment the election was made unanimous and the Convention stood and sang Gloria in Excelsis as an act of thanksgiving for the harmorious outcome of the convention's business. After passing resolutions of thanks to the President and the Rector and Vestry of St. James and after appointing a committee of three clergymen and three laymen headed by Dr. Foley to notify Dr. Manning of his election, Convention adjourned.

A week before Christmas Dr. Foley received the following letter

(8)

from Dr. Manning written from St. Agnes Vicarage under date of December 16:

"Since the time, now nearly two weeks ago, when I was notified by you and the members of your committee of my election as Bishop of the Diocese of Harrisburg, I have given my whole thought to the call to this most sacred office, and have asked only to be guided to whatever decision was right and for the truest interests of the Church.

"I have tried to look at the matter from every possible point of view and have taken time for full consideration, and it is now my clear conviction that it is my duty to continue in my present field of labor.

"I write these words with very sincere regret, not only because your Diocese will be put to further trouble, but also because the more I have studied the facts in regard to it, the more its conditions and its opportunities have appealed to me and attracted me.

"Believing, however, that my decision is a right one, and praying for the work of your Diocese God's truest blessing, I am

Faithfully yours,
William T. Manning."

So, more travail lay ahead before the Diocese of Harrisburg could really come to birth.

III

Two days after Christmas, the Standing Committee met in Harrisburg to arrange for the calling of a special convention for the election of a Bishop. This convention met in St. Stephen's Church, Harrisburg, on Tuesday evening, January 31. The Rev. Mr. Baker having again been elected President, the Convention proceeded with the business of placing nominations for Bishop. This time, no local men were put in nomination. Those who were named included the Rev. Messrs. F. F. Reese, James Henry Darlington, Paul Matthews, Charles F. Williams, William F. Faber, and W. H. Van Allen.

When Convention began balloting next morning, it was apparent that the contest was between Darlington and Matthews. From the first ballot, Dr. Darlington was elected on every ballot by the laity; on ballots Four through Seven, Paul Matthews was elected by the clergy—indeed, he remained the preference of the clergy until the twelfth ballot. On the thirteenth ballot, the clergy yielded to the laity and Dr. Darlington received a majority of the votes in both orders. On motion of the Rev. William Dorwart, the election was made unanimous—a motion which Convention passed by a rising vote. After singing Gloria in Excelsis as an act of thanksgiving for the harmonious result, Convention adjourned.

A committee under the chairmanship of the Rev. Walter R. Breed went to Brooklyn to notify Dr. Darlington of his election. By February 7, they had received his letter of acceptance. A month later, the Standing Committee met in Harrisburg and arranged for the consecration to take place in Christ Church, Brooklyn, of which Dr. Darlington was then Rector.

The service of consecration was held on Wednesday morning, April 26. Participating from this Diocese were Rev. Charles Morrison, President of the Standing Committee, who read the certificate of election; and Mr. C. M. Clement, Secretary of the Diocese, who read the testimonials of the Convention. The consecrators were the three Pennsylvania Bishops—Whitaker of Pennsylvania, Talbot of Central Pennsylvania, and Whitehead of Pittsburgh.

The new Bishop was 49 years old. He had made a brilliant record in the Newark High School, New York University and Princeton. It was at the latter institution that he trained for the ministry earning his Ph. D. degree meanwhile in the graduate school. Upon graduation from Princeton, he was called by Dr. Partridge to be his assistant at Christ Church, Brooklyn. Upon the death of Dr. Partridge in 1882, Dr. Darlington was unanimously elected Rector. During his twenty-three years of tenure, the church made notable progress both materially and spiritually. The Rector not only identified himself prominently with the affairs of the Diocese of Long Island where for a time he was Archdeacon of Northern Brooklyn, but was prominent in the civic, music, literary, cultural and patriotic life of the city. An editorial in the Brooklyn "Eagle" written at the time of his consecration indicates the esteem in which he was held

(10)

and attests the wisdom of the Diocese in calling him to be its first chief pastor.

"There will be regret within church circles because of the Rev. Dr. Darlington's acceptance of the Bishopric of Harrisburg, as it will involve his removal from this community to whose better activities and to whose moral and spiritual interests he has been conscientiously devoted. The testimony will be general to the benignity of his life, to the sincerity of his piety, to his unselfish devotion to the interests of his parish, and to his sincere support of every movement for religious and ethical uplift within the circle of his influence.

"He is loved by his church, respected by our citizenship, and regarded with high esteem by all the moral, literary and finer social circles which here exist. We think he has in him the making of an efficient Bishop. He is not only a man of piety but of judgment, of moderation, of gentle temper and commendable tact. He has the qualities, in short, which make a Bishop acceptable, useful and successful as a Diocesan force, not only within his jurisdiction, but within the circles of Christianity at large.

"Every one who knows him is his friend. He has not an enemy nor an ill-wisher in the world. He will go into a Diocese which he can make into his own likeness, as he will be its first Bishop. The Episcopal Church is by no means the strongest one in that Diocese, but the number of its parishes is increasing and the number of their communicants constantly show an encouraging growth. The other Protestant denominations in the territory which the Diocese comprises will, we are sure, be glad to meet Bishop Darlington, and will find him sympathetic with their best interests and efforts."

The day following his consecration, Bishop Darlington came to Harrisburg where a reception was held for him that evening in the auditorium of the Board of Trade attended by the religious and civic leaders of the city. Commenting on this meeting, the Harrisburg "Patriot" said:

"The ever-growing fellowship of man and brotherhood of Christ was well illustrated last night in the great outpour-

ing of the men and women of this city, representing every
sect and denomination, to welcome Dr. James Henry Darlington, the first Bishop of the new Diocese of Harrisburg.

"Such a gathering was never before seen in this city. It
was a fitting testimony to the esteem which the Bishop's
abilities, scholarship and piety have won for him."

Thus, under these happy auspices, the men who conceived the Diocese
of Harrisburg saw their dream translated into reality.

Chapter Two

THE DIOCESE OF HARRISBURG

I

It does not require much imagination to believe that when Dr. Darlington was informed of his election as Bishop of the Diocese of Harrisburg, he spent as much time as he could spare from his parochial duties in familiarizing himself with the area in which he was soon to be the chief pastor. Taking a map of Pennsylvania, he would naturally plot out the limits of his Diocese. Beginning at the southeastern tip of Lancaster County, he would run his pencil along the historic Mason and Dixon Line till he reached the southwestern border of Bedford County; then, turning north, he would trace the western boundaries of Bedford, Blair, Centre, Clinton and Potter Counties; turning east at the northwest corner of Potter County, he would trace a jagged line, following the northwest corner of Potter, Tioga, Sullivan, Columbia, Dauphin and Lancaster Counties till he reached the place where his pencil had started. Within this irregular trapezoid were 24 of Pennsylxania's 67 counties: Potter, Tioga, Sullivan, Clinton, Lycoming, Montour, Columbia, Centre, Union, Snyder, Northumberland, Blair, Huntingdon, Mifflin, Juniata, Perry, Dauphin, Cumberland, Bedford, Fulton, Franklin, Adams, York and Lancaster.

The census figures for 1900 showed that this large area contained a population of 1,072,281. There was no great concentration of population, only four cities—Harrisburg, Lancaster, York and Altoona had a population greater than 30,000. Thus it was a rural diocese over which he was being called upon to preside. Since the Episcopal Church has been traditionally an urban church, it would be necessary to provide clergy who were missionary-minded—men who could minister to farmers, miners, tanners, lumberjacks, iron workers and railroaders, as well as to business executives and professional men. Moreover, he would have to find means to make the work attractive enough to keep them from becoming discouraged and moving to more promising fields. As he was to learn, it was because this had not been done that many parishes which should have been well established were still struggling to maintain themselves.

Immigration had shifted from northwestern to southeastern Europe. This meant that the church could not rely on the coming of English people into the Diocese to strengthen the churches as it had in the past, but the church would have to look for its growth to natural increase and to missionary enterprise. In general, each community was able to absorb its labor supply so that young people were not obliged to seek employment outside their home towns. This would give a certain stability to a congregation and insure a continuity of leadership from generation to generation. It was preponderately a white population. Only in Harrisburg was there a sufficient concentration of negroes to present a challenge to the church. The possibility of work among students was suggested by the fact that five of the state's thirteen Normal Schools were located within the Diocese; beside this, there were nine colleges and a bevy of private academies in operation. While only the Yates School at Lancaster was under the auspices of the church, there were Episcopal students in all these institutions who could profit by the church's ministry.

Though the church would have to make its way in a region predominantly conservative, Protestant and Evangelical, their influence in maintaining the tradition of the Puritan Sabbath could be a distinct advantage to the church. Weak churches could be combined into circuits since people did not all insist on having a morning service at eleven o'clock but were willing to attend afternoon or evening services.

II

Having made this general survey of the territory in which he was to work, the Bishop-elect would next turn to a study of the places in which the church was at work, and he would give some attention to the routes by which he could most conveniently make his parish visitations. Harrisburg seemed the natural place in which to set up his base of operations. It was the capital of the state; railroads led out of the city in all directions and the church here was well established. St. Stephen's had been an incorporated parish since 1826; the Primary Convention of the Diocese of Central Pennsylvania had been held there in 1871, and it was in St. Stephen's that he had been elected Bishop. The missionary spirit of the parish was attested by the fact that in 1899 it established All Saint's Mission in a lunch room

(14)

on Race Street near a cigar factory. The clergy of St. Stephen's with the assistance of one of the Sisters of the Order of St. John Baptist and later by a deaconess, developed the work until 1901 the mission was obliged to seek larger quarters and it had good prospects of becoming a parish. St. Paul's, in the west end of the city, had been incorporated since 1859. It had gotten off to a slow start but since the Reverend LeRoy F. Baker became Rector in 1880, the parish had grown in number and influence, which influence it was seeking to extend by the establishment of St. Andrew's Chapel on Allison's Hill.

In determining to make Harrisburg the See City, Dr. Darlington was not unmindful of the claims of Williamsport to that honor. The people of Williamsport had taken a prominent part in the movement for the establishment of the Diocese; two of the Williamsport clergy had been serious contenders for the office of Bishop; it was a beautiful city, bordering the West Branch of the Susquehanna, set amid the everlasting hills with a delightful summer climate; like Harrisburg, it was a railroad center and would afford an excellent base from which to visit the parishes in the northwestern part of his Diocese. Furthermore, Williamsport was the strongest center of the church in the Diocese, for the city boasted four incorporated parishes. The Christ Church, in the downtown section, had been incorporated since 1847; Trinity Church, near the station and the famous Park Hotel, had been established in 1866; at the west end of the city, All Saints' was a new parish having been established in 1901, and at the east end, St. Mary's had been at work since 1895. It seemed fitting, therefore, to make Williamsport the See City during the summer months.

In planning for his parish visitations, railroad time tables and not road maps would have to be consulted. Many of the parishes could be reached in comparative comfort by using the main line of the Pennsylvania or its subsidiaries, then known as the Northern Central and the Philadelphia and Erie. These roads provided fast and frequent service and many of the trains were equipped with parlor, dining and sleeping cars. To reach other points, he would have to ride on branch roads where the service was less frequent and the equipment more primitive. In several instances, he would have to use narrow gauge railroads where the equipment was reminiscent of the early days of railroading. The rural trolley line could serve in

(15)

visiting parishes adjacent to the cities in the eastern part of the Diocese. It was evident that his visitations would involve a great deal of time and considerable fatigue.

Going east on the Main Line, en route to Lancaster, he could visit Trinity Mission at Steelton, St. Michael and All Angels' Mission at Middletown, and St. Luke's Mission at Mt. Joy. The two parishes in Lancaster were among the strongest in the Diocese. St. James had been established since 1744 and had a long and distinguished history; St. John's, organized one hundred and ten years later as a protest against the prevailing practice of supporting the church by pew rent, served the people in the west end of Lancaster and was known as St. John's Free Church. In the rural district east of Lancaster to be reached by trolley, was Bangor Church at Churchtown, the site of the oldest work in the Diocese, the church having started there in 1733; Christ Church, Leacock, incorporated as a parish in 1810; All Saints', Paradise, incorporated in 1842; and Grace Church, Nickel Mines, chartered in 1860. Going north from Lancaster on the Reading, he could reach St. Paul's, Manheim, incorporated in 1870, and Hope Church, Mount Hope, which had been established in 1849. Going south from Lancaster on the Columbia Branch of the Pennsylvania he could visit St. Paul's, Columbia. While there had been a parish there since 1849, the work dated back to pre-Revolutionary days. From here he could take a train home, following the north bank of the Susquehanna, stopping, meanwhile, to visit St. John's Marietta—a parish which had existed since 1866.

Another swing around the circle from Harrisburg would take him to York on the Northern Central. York had been a center of church activities from colonial times. Historic old St. John's had been a parish since 1785 and its clergy had exerted an influence both in the councils of the Dioceses of Pennsylvania and Central Pennsylvania. In 1905 it supported three chapels in the city—St. Andrew's Chapel, the Chapel of the Incarnation and Chapel of Ease. A ride on one of Pennsylvania's "short lines"—The Maryland and Pennsylvania (popularly referred to in York County as the "Mom and Pop") would enable him to visit St. David's Mission at Delta. This mission was in the formative stage, having been started by St. John's, York, in 1899, and was then having regular Wednesday evening services in the basement of Lloyd's Hall. The Western Maryland

(16)

could take him from York to Gettysburg where he could visit the Church of the Prince of Peace which had been an organized mission since 1903, and to Blue Ridge Summit where the Church of the Transfiguration had been an organized mission since 1892. The recently organized mission at Beartown, known as Calvary Church, could be conveniently visited from Blue Ridge Summit as could the struggling St. Stephen's Mission at Waynesboro. Taking a branch of the Cumberland Valley at Waynesboro, he could visit Trinity parish at Chambersburg which had been established since 1869. Going south from there, he could visit St. James' Mission at Greencastle; then, going north on the main line of the Cumberland Valley, he could visit the newly organized St. Andrew's Mission at Shippensburg, historic St. John's, Carlisle, whose charter dates from 1821, and St. Luke's Mission at Mechanicsburg before returning to Harrisburg.

The main line of the Pennsylvania would take him into the western part of the Diocese. He would stop to visit Nativity, Newport, where work had been going on for twenty years but which had only been an organized mission since 1902; he would stop at Thompsontown to visit St. Stephen's which had been an incorporated parish since 1825, with its quaint stone church set in the midst of a quiet countryside. St. Mark's, Lewistown, was one of the more important parishes in this part of the Diocese. It had been established in 1824 and was visited by Bishop White on his western trip in 1826. Changing cars at Mt. Union, he would take the narrow gauge East Broadtop Railroad to make the ten mile trip to visit Trinity Mission at Rock Hill Furnace (Orbisonia) where the church had a ministry to the miners. Returning to Mount Union he would continue west to Huntingdon to visit the old parish of St. John established in 1820. Taking the Huntingdon and Broadtop, he would make a side trip to Bedford to visit St. James which had been incorporated since 1866. Returning to Huntingdon, he would visit Trinity Mission which had been at work for several years in Tyrone, before going on to Altoona to visit St. Luke's, established in 1858—just eight years after the Pennsylvania Railroad had laid out the town. Returning to Tyrone, branch lines would take him to two old and well established parishes. St. Paul's, Philipsburg, was chartered in 1827 and is said to have been the first church in the country to be lighted by electricity. St. John's in Bellefonte was incorporated in 1839 and was, in 1905, one of the larger parishes in the western part of the Diocese.

(17)

The Northern Central would take him into the northwestern part of the Diocese. Changing cars at Millersburg, he would go up the Lykens Valley to visit Christ Church, Lykens, which had been incorporated in 1872, and Christ Mission at Williamstown. Continuing north to Sunbury, he would want to visit St. Matthew's—a parish which had been established in 1827 and the home parish of Mr. Charles M. Clement, Secretary of the Diocese. A trolley trip across the river would bring him to Selinsgrove where All Saints' Mission had been struggling to exist for some thirty years and was then in one of its happier periods. From Sunbury, he could visit Trinity Church, Shamokin, established in 1866, and Trinity Church, Centralia, founded two years later. On his return to Sunbury, he could stop to see the work being done at St. Stephen's Mission in Mount Carmel. Up the North Branch from Sunbury, work was being carried on in all the river towns. St. John's parish had been established in Catawissa in 1872. At Berwick, Christ Mission had been started about the turn of the century, and there were old and well established parishes at Bloomsburg, Danville and Northumberland. St. Paul's, Bloomsburg, was founded in 1793; Christ Memorial in Danville in 1828; and St. Mark's, Northumberland, in 1848. St. Gabriel's at Coles Creek was a strictly rural parish incorporated in 1877.

Assuming that some of the visits would be made out of Williamsport, we will survey the work in the northern part of the Diocese from that point. He could visit the Church of Our Saviour at Montoursville—a parish established in 1870—by trolley. The Reading would take him to Muncy to visit St. James which had been in existence since 1820. From Muncy, he could visit the organized mission of the Good Shepherd in Upper Fairfield and then go north to visit St. John's Missions in the summer resorts of Eaglesmere and LaPorte.

A short trip east on the Philadelphia and Erie would enable him to visit two old but not too flourishing parishes. Christ Church, Milton, had been founded in 1793 and St. James Church, Exchange, had been established in 1849.

Heading northwest on the P. & E. he would stop at the newly organized Trinity Mission at Jersey Shore; at St. Paul's, Lock Haven, where the parish had been in existence since 1857; then on to Renovo to see Trinity Church which had been incorporated as a parish in 1901. From here, by a very tedious journey, he could reach the farthest

(18)

outpost of the Diocese—Christ Church, Coudersport, incorporated as a parish in 1880; and the beautiful church at Brookland, perhaps the most beautiful small church in the Diocese.

The church had been established in Tioga County since 1841 when St. Paul's Church was founded at Wellsboro. Twenty years later, St. Andrew's, Tioga, was chartered as a parish. In 1869, two new parishes were established in the county—St. Luke's, Blossburg, and St. James, Mansfield. Trinity, Antrim, was incorporated in 1882 and there were missions at Arnot, Lawrenceville and Westfield. To reach this remote corner of the Diocese involved tedious travel. To reach Mansfield and Blossburg, it was necessary to take the Pennsylvania to Elmira and double back on the Erie. To reach the other towns meant taking the Fallbrook Branch of the New York Central and making two changes to reach Westfield, while Wellsboro, Lawrenceville and Tioga could be reached without change of cars.

The trips which we have suggested could have been made just as they appear. In practice, however, it would be quite unlikely that a Bishop would find it possible to devise any such schedule. We have outlined these imaginary trips in order to make clear the areas where the church was at work in the Diocese and we have been at pains to indicate routes of travel so that the Bishop's travel problems before the days of the automobile could be better appreciated. While it may be monotonous to read the dates when the several parishes were incorporated, they do give some indication of how well the church was established in the Diocese. The reader who has followed this itinerary carefully will have noticed that the church was at work in each of the twenty-four counties with the exception of Fulton and Union.

III

While it was over a new Diocese that Bishop Darlington would preside, the church had been at work in the territory for more than a century and a half. Before the Revolution, the land now lying within the bounds of the Diocese of Harrisburg was a frontier region. East of the Susquehanna, the town of Lancaster, laid out in 1730, was the center of a well settled community, and, for a time, the town could boast of being the largest inland town in the Country. West of the Susquehanna, there were small settlements at York, Shippensburg and Carlisle. In the Heart of the Alleghenies, along "the old Forbes

(19)

road," a considerable settlement clustered around Fort Bedford—an important center of defense after 1750. At the junction of the North and West Branches of the Susquehanna, Sunbury and Northumberland had been laid out in 1772, while far up the Juniata, Huntingdon had existed since 1767. The white men who lived in this country were Indian traders, pioneers who had received land grants from the Penns, squatters who defied the claims of the proprietors, and British soldiers who sought to defend the land from the pretensions of the French established at Fort Duquesne. They traveled by canoe or over Indian trails; they lived in lonely log cabins or behind stockades; the Indian war whoop was a familiar sound that instinctively brought their muskets to the shoulder.

East of the Susquehanna, the Indian menace was never far removed. In 1744, an important treaty conference was held in the Lancaster Courthouse from June 22 to July 4, attended by the Lieutenant-Governor of the Province; Commissioners from Maryland and Virginia; Conrad Weiser, the famous trader and Interpreter; and by deputies from the Onondagas, Senecas, Cayugas, Oneidas and Tuscaroras. After the outbreak of the French and Indian War, the Indian menace became more acute. As a means of protection, the people of Lancaster built a blockhouse and stockade in 1755. A midnight alarm, happily false, once brought three hundred citizens into the streets with their fifty guns. Throughout the war, Lancaster suffered from Indian thievery and minor depredations and in 1763 some of the vengeful whites fell upon a band of friendly Conastogas and massacred all but fifteen who were taken to Lancaster and lodged in the workhouse for protection. While Christmas services were being held at St. James the "Paxton Boys" rode into Lancaster and dragged the hapless Indians from prison and killed them in cold blood. A happier side of Indian relations is revealed by the gracious invitation of the Reverend Thomas Barton, missionary at Carlisle, to the Indians who had come there to trade to attend divine service. Many of the Indians came and, had not hostilities broken out, a fruitful mission to the Indians might have begun. When Mr. Barton moved to Lancaster, Sir William Johnson, Superintendent of Indian Affairs in North America, sent his half-breed son to Lancaster to be under his guidance and instruction.

There were some members of the Church in every town, but they were too few to attract and support the services of a resident clergyman. The fact that they were not deprived of the Church's ministry altogether is due to the support and interest of the Society for the Propagation of the Gospel in Foreign Parts. This Society owes its origin to the vision and enthusiasm of the Reverend Thomas Bray. He was appointed Commissary to Maryland in 1696, and after spending a year or so in the colonies, returned and interested the Archbishop of Canterbury in the plight of the settlers in those colonies where the Church did not receive public support. As a result, the S. P. G. or London Society was chartered in 1701 and, through its efforts, scattered congregations were gathered together and new outposts of the Church were established.

To make a preliminary survey of the field, the Society sent the Reverend George Ieith to America. He reported that, except in Philadelphia, there was no clergyman of the Church resident in Pennsylvania. Reverend Robert Weyman was sent to Pennsylvania in 1719. He ministered to a wide parish. Of interest to our present discussion, is a letter to the Society dated October 1, 1726, in which he states that he often travelled to Churchtown and preached to Episcopalians there. The homes of the settlers being too small to accommodate the congregations, services were held in the open under the shade of the trees. Under the guidance of the Reverend Griffith Hughes, Bangor Church was built in 1733. Thus Bangor Church, Churchtown, is the oldest parish in the Diocese and continues to this day to serve the Church in the eastern end of Lancaster County.

In 1744, the Reverend Richard Locke, a missionary of the Society, happened to be in Lancaster. The churchmen who lived there prevailed upon him to remain with them and organize a congregation. He acceded to their wishes and, on October 3, 1744, St. James parish was formally organized. The congregation worshipped in the Courthouse where they had been wont to meet for services whenever a priest of the Church happened to be in town. During his stay in Lancaster, Mr. Locke also ministered to the congregation at Bangor Church and sometimes visited families as far away as York. Relations with his Lancaster flock were not happy, so, in 1748, he resigned and was licensed by the Bishop of London for work in Virginia. The people of Lancaster and vicinity were without a clergyman till the spring of 1751 when the Reverend George Craig took charge of the work. During his ministry, the congregation of St. James built a stone church on the site of the present church. Finding conditions in Lancaster not to his liking, he asked the Society to transfer him to Chester and he left in 1758.

Meanwhile, the Reverend Thomas Barton had been sent by the Society to be missionary to the congregations in York and Cumberland Counties. He had three parishes to which he ministered regularly and which were organized with wardens and vestries. The largest of the three congregations was at Huntington (about three and a half miles west of the present York Springs) where there was a glebe for the Rector, and where Mr. Barton officiated three Sundays out of every six. He ministered at Carlisle two Sundays in six, and once every six weeks at York where the population was largely German. Mr. Barton had the spirit of the true missionary. His attempt to make friends with the Indians has already been mentioned. Four times a year, he visited the people of Shippensburg and Harrisburg as well as the scattered families in the district. He was a true shepherd of his flock. When the news of Braddock's defeat reached Carlisle, he put himself at the head of his people and was prepared day or night to answer the alarm and lead them against the advancing Indians. When General Forbes was ordered to march on Fort Duquesne, he offered his services as chaplain and accompanied the troops on the expedition. On his return to Carlisle, the Society transferred him to Lancaster where he remained as Rector for nineteen years. With Christian fortitude he carried forward his work despite frail health and an inadequate salary. Not only do the churches in Lancaster and Churchtown stand in his debt, but St. Thomas, Morgantown, in the Diocese of Bethlehem and St. John's, Pequea, in the Diocese of Pennsylvania. There is evidence to show that the first work in Columbia was initiated by Mr. Barton. The approach of the Revolution was very embarrassing to the missionary. He was bound by an oath of loyalty both to the King and to the Society. St. James had many patriots among its leading members. After independence was declared, Mr. Barton's position became intolerable. He could not, in good conscience, omit the prayers for the King and the Royal Family from the service, and such prayers were, of course, unacceptable to the patriotic wing of his congregation. While awaiting the outcome of events, he held no public services but ministered privately to the sick and the distressed in their homes. With Howe's evacuation of Philadelphia, Mr. Barton deemed it wise to seek asylum in New York; in the meantime, his wife and family were harbored by

(22)

a family in Churchtown. Worn out by the sufferings connected with his exile, discouraged by separation from his family, and overcome by physical weakness, he died in New York in 1789 at the age of fifty. He stands without peer as a representative of the London Society in America.

The Society did not forget the churches in Cumberland County with Mr. Barton's removal to Lancaster. The Reverend William Thomson took charge in 1760 and remained till 1769; he was succeeded in quick order by John Andrews, Daniel Botwell, and John Campbell. Mr. Campbell did not seem to have the political scruples of Mr. Barton, and was able to continue his work during the Revolution and remained at Carlisle till 1804.

While the clergy at Carlisle served the church at York, St. John's has special historic associations since the town of York was the Federal capital during the winter of 1777-78. With Howe's occupation of Philadelphia, the Continental Congress at first fled to Lancaster, and feeling safer with the Susquehanna River between them and the British, they removed to York. While there, the Articles of Confederation were under consideration and finally adopted. Many of the members of Congress belonged to the Church of England and it is certain that they worshipped at St. John's during their stay in York. On a visit to York, General Washington went to St. John's one Sunday to worship, but he got only as far as the front door since the minister was serving at Carlisle that day. Colonel Thomas Hartley and Major John B. Clark, Revolutionary officers, are buried in St. John's churchyard. General Gates' headquarters was not far from the church and he was challenged to fight a duel behind it. In 1774, the Queen of England presented the parish with a bell, but since the church had neither belfry nor tower, it was deposited on the pavement of Joseph Updegraf in Center Square, where it remained for some time. When the news of the Declaration of Independence reached York, a group of patriots, among whom was James Smith, one of the signers of the Declaration, hoisted the bell to the cupola of the courthouse where it rang out the glad news far and wide. It was this bell that summoned the members of the Continental Congress to their meetings while they sat at York. When the State House was torn down in 1841, the church authorities seized the bell despite popular protest and hid it beneath the church till the clamor died down.

(23)

A tower and belfry having been erected, the bell was hung in its intended place. Shortly afterward, it cracked and was sent to Baltimore to be recast. In 1901, it cracked again while tolling for the death of President McKinley and was once more recast. It cracked a third time in 1910 and has since occupied an honored place within the church, and well it might, for next to the Liberty Bell, it is the most famous bell in the country.

Central Pennsylvania did not develop economically till the first half of the nineteenth century. As a result of the exploitation of its iron, lumber, coal, and limestone; because of the construction of the Pennsylvania Canal, and later, the coming of the railroad, many hamlets grew into thriving towns. As we have seen, the church was established in a few of them before 1850.

After the Revolution, the Episcopal Church was faced with a critical situation. Many of the ablest clergy had returned to England; by many extreme patriots, it was considered a "Tory" church. At a time when the Methodists were sending their circuit riders into the frontier to minister to the pioneer, the Episcopal Church was obliged to reassemble its forces and perfect its organization. As a result, church families in the "back country" often joined other communions. We have no space here to give the details of the history of the parishes established before 1860. We can only observe that they owe their existence to the devotion of a congregation which was determined, at all costs, to have a minister; to the missionary zeal of some neighboring parish priest; or to some patron who built a church and gathered his workers about him as a congregation. We have no wish to slight the parishes which came into existence in the first part of the nineteenth century at the expense of the pre-Revolutionary parishes. We have given space to them to emphasize the debt the Diocese owes to the London Society and its intrepid missionaries, and to point up the fact that the Diocese was at one time a missionary field.

After the Civil War, parishes multiplied more rapidly. This growth was due to the same causes that had operated earlier, but more particularly to the activities of the several General Missionaries who were at work between 1876 and 1903. The idea of an itinerant missionary was suggested by Bishop Howe to the Convention of 1872. It was his opinion, that if funds were available, six such missionaries could be profitably employed, and that their work would result in the doubling of the number of parishes in the Diocese. Nothing was done, however, till 1876, when the Board of Missions authorized the appointment of two itinerants. For this work the Bishop named the Reverend Thomas O. Tongue and the Reverend J. McAlpine Harding. Mr. Tongue had his base at Harrisburg and worked west along the main line of the Pennsylvania as far as Tyrone and Hollidaysburg, while Mr. Harding was to work out of Athens into Sullivan, Bradford and Columbia Counties. In 1879, Mr. Tongue shifted his base to Huntingdon. Both men resigned by 1880 and were succeeded by men who remained on the job for only a short time. The project was abandoned in 1882 and not revived until 1884 when the Bishop appointed the Reverend Samuel P. Kelly to be General Missionary for the whole Diocese. He was supported by offerings from the Sunday School taken from Septuagesima to Easter. He attacked his work with such zeal that, by 1890, the task was beyond the ability of any single man to carry. It was then determined that each Archdeaconry should employ its own General Missionary and support him through the offerings of the Sunday School. Only the Archdeaconry of Scranton acted on this suggestion for a brief time. Bishop Talbot revived the office in 1898 and, after two false starts, the Reverend Reginald Radcliffe assumed the position in 1901 and was at work at the time of the division of the Diocese.

As a result of the labors of these men, almost forgotten mission stations were reopened; dead parishes were revitalized; new fields of opportunity were discovered; and scattered congregations were brought together. To the labors of these men we owe the churches at LaPorte, Eaglesmere, Selinsgrove, Orbisonia, and Tyrone. The old stone church at Thompsontown, vacant for half a century, was reopened and a promising work was established; new centers were explored in Juniata County at McAllisterville and Richfield; while St. John's, Huntingdon, was given a new lease of life. One wonders what might have been the result had the Diocese shared Bishop Howe's vision.

When the American Episcopal Church was organized after the Revolution, the state became the Diocese of Pennsylvania. The convention elected as first Bishop of the Diocese, the Reverend William White, Rector of Christ Church, Philadelphia, who became the second

(25)

Bishop to be consecrated for the Church. As Rector of Christ Church, he had been sympathetic with the patriot cause and he had been a leader in rallying the Churchmen of the Middle States after the treaty with England. The "Proposed Book" of 1785 was largely his work. After his election as Bishop, he continued to serve as Rector of Christ Church, and it is evident that, with travel conditions as they were, he could give this vast territory only scant Episcopal oversight. No records of his visitations are available before 1811, but it may be safely assumed that they were confined to Philadelphia and its immediate vicinity. In 1813, he visited Lancaster and York. In 1814 he paid a visit to northeastern Pennsylvania, during which St. Matthews Church, Bradford County, was constituted. On a visit to Lancaster in 1820, to consecrate the new St. James Church, he brought with him a young protege who was about to be ordained to the Priesthood, the Rev. William Augustus Muhlenberg. Muhlenberg became Co-Rector of the parish the following December and immediately infused new life into the parish. He was responsible for starting St. James Sunday School, the first such project in the Diocese, for the public schools of Lancaster, for St. James Dispensary, and he initiated the work at Harrisburg which grew into St. Stephen's Church. Muhlenberg's name is known throughout the Church as a pioneer in the movement for Church boarding schools of which his "Flushing Institute" was a pattern and inspiration, for the idea of the "institutional church," and for the famous Muhlenberg Memorial presented to the House of Bishops in 1853. We know him today for his Christmas hymn

"Shout the glad tidings, exultingly sing,
Jerusalem triumphs, Messiah is King."

The Diocese may well be proud of the fact that one who was so well known in the Church was, in his early ministry, one of its clergy.

Lancaster was regarded as the western limit of the Diocese, for York was not revisited until 1822. In 1825, the Bishop got as far west as Lewistown on a projected trip to Pittsburgh, but, after fracturing his wrist, he returned to Philadelphia. He made the trip successfully in 1826 and we may assume that he visited several congregations within our present Diocese. In 1827, the Reverend Henry U. Onderdonk was elected Bishop-Coadjutor, and since he had no parochial responsibilities, the remoter parts of the Diocese must have received more Episcopal supervision. Bishop White served both the

(26)

Diocese and Christ Church until his death in 1836. He was active in the civic life of Philadelphia, thus enhancing the prestige of the Church and breaking down some of the prejudice under which it suffered. He was one of the founders of the Philadelphia Bible Society—the first such society in the country and the forerunner of the American Bible Society. In 1812, he was associated with some of the clergy of his Diocese in founding the Society for the Advancement of Christianity in Pennsylvania. The Society's object was the support of missionaries in the remoter parts of the state. Bishop Darlington applied to this Society again and again for aid in carrying on his missionary work. It is also interesting to note that one of the prominent members of this society in the early days was the Reverend Jackson Kemper, then Bishop White's assistant at Christ Church and later to become the first Missionary Bishop to the Northwest.

Bishop Onderdonk had an unhappy Episcopate. His election was held in the midst of a sharp controversy between the new High Church Party and those who called themselves Evangelicals. While Bishop White was no partisan, he had little sympathy with what he regarded as the pious pretensions of the Evangelicals. When editing the Diocesan Journals for publication in 1824, he deleted from the parochial reports the passages that referred to the supposedly superior spiritual condition of the Evangelical parishes. While the Bishop had too much personal prestige to be attacked directly, the Evangelicals made an indirect attack by organizing an independent missionary society over which he could exercise but little control, and the clergy sent their candidates for Holy Orders to the Virginia Seminary where they would not be influenced by the High Church Professors who taught at General. Acceding to what he believed was the wish of his Diocese, Bishop White asked for relief. The two parties were so evenly balanced that the special convention called to elect a Coadjutor in 1826 adjourned in a deadlock. At the Convention of 1827, Mr. Onderdonk was elected by a close vote as a compromise candidate. The Evangelicals insisted that his election would not have been possible had not some of the clergy of their party been declared ineligible to vote.

While passions cooled somewhat so that Bishop Onderdonk could quietly succeed Bishop White on his death in 1836, the bitterness engendered by his election continued to smoulder. In the 1840's, the American Church was sharply divided by the Oxford Movement.

(27)

Writing of the proponents of the Oxford Movement Professor James Thayer Addison says:

"In these early forties the men most affected by the Tracts were certain of the younger clergy and the students of the General Theological Seminary. The enthusiasm for monastic asceticism which led Breck, Adams and the junior Hobart to temporary celibacy in the wilds of Wisconsin was but one response of many in the rising generation. It had already begun to be noticeable that they differed from the numerous representatives of the older High Churchmanship on at least one important point. The latter, like their seventeenth century models, did not wince at the appelation "Protestant"; they heartily commended the Reformation; and they believed that the Episcopal Church in the United States was so nearly perfect that it could hardly be improved upon. But the younger converts of Newman and Pusey were inclined to be apologetic about the deplorable condition of a Church which had so nearly forgotten its Catholic heritage. For them the Reformation was a deformation; and the ancient Church of Rome instead of being a target for their abuse, began to exert upon them an uneasy fascination."

The Evangelical point of view is well presented in a Convention address made by our own Bishop Potter after some of the bitterness had gone out of the Controversy.

"We may well mourn that instead of accepting the Reformation as a blessing and planting themselves on the liberty and the simplicity of the doctrine which that event gave back to the Church, men of thoughtful minds and devout lives can be found who pine after the spiritual bondage and the superstitious worship which our fathers were unable to bear . . . . . Should we ever come to hanker after the private confessional and the sacrament of penance, after more power and less responsibility for the clergy, and more responsibility and less liberty for the people—in such case we should know that we are in imminent danger."

Bishop Onderdork's sympathies were with the friends of the Oxford Movement, and as the Evangelical Party became stronger, his position became more difficult. His Convention presented him for drunkenness, hoping to embassass him by forcing him to stand trial. The canons provided that a Bishop might avoid a trial either by confessing his guilt or resigning his jurisdiction. The Bishop tried both expedients. He explained that he had taken to the use of spirits on the advice of his doctor in order to try to relieve a chronic stomach ailment but had given it up when he discovered the effect it had upon him, and he offered to resign. The Convention refused to accept his resignation hoping to force the trial. Meantime, General Convention passed a canon allowing a Bishop to resign to the House of Bishops without the consent of his Diocese. Taking advantage of this provision, he presented his resignation to the House of Bishops and confessed his intemperance. But his brethren proved no more merciful than his Convention and he was indefinitely suspended from his office. The sentence was remitted in 1856, but he was never restored to his jurisdiction.

The third Bishop of Pennsylvania was the Reverend Alonzo Potter, Vice President of Union College at Schenectady, and Professor of Moral Philosophy and Political Economy there. Though but forty-five years old, he had a reputation throughout the Church as a speaker and educator. He was a leader in the temperance movement that was getting underway in America, and he was in sympathy with the Evangelical wing of the Church, though he was never a strong partisan. These facts, no doubt, were instrumental in his election, and though he had many strong ties at Union, pressure both from within and without the Diocese was exerted upon him to accept his election and he was consecrated in 1845.

The new Bishop's reaction to conditions in Pennsylvania is reflected in part of a letter he wrote to a friend in Boston:

"I have been at home now for about ten days after an eight weeks' tour in western Pennsylvania and along the northern and eastern frontiers of the State. The weather was delightful, the country is surprisingly fine, and the inhabitants were to me all that I could have possibly asked. Our Churches, however, are very feeble; the clergy struggling to live on inadequate stipends, and great mountains of prejudice built up by ignorance without and by our own unfaithfulness and divisions within. A Diocesan of Penn-

(29)

sylvania must calculate at best upon great trial and sore discouragements. At present, we are at peace so far as I am concerned, and devoutly do I pray that we may remain so. But I cannot be blind to the times in which we are fallen, and to the impossibility of giving satisfaction to everybody."

The Bishop neither avoided the hard trial nor succumbed to the sore discouragement. It may be stated that he came as near as humanly possible to satisfying everybody during the twenty-one years of his leadership. Clergy of all parties were made to feel at home, and the peace which attended his coming remained throughout his life. He took an active interest in missions, and, after years of patience, succeeded in bringing the two missionary societies of his Diocese together, resulting in more efficient management and more generous support of the work. He sought to raise the standard of education in the Sunday Schools, urging the larger parishes to establish training courses from which teachers in the small parishes might profit. To improve the morale of the clergy, he gathered them in convocations to inspire them to continue in their intellectual and spiritual growth. He carefully supervised all candidates for Holy Orders and gave them counsel which has not become out dated:

"A minister cannot *grow* in power and edification without *systematic* study of the Bible, of theology, and of moral philosophy. That there is so little of this study now among our ministers is one great reason why so few of them *improve* after the first few years."

Among the institutions which owe much to him is the Episcopal Academy which he had reopened, the Seaman's Institute, the Episcopal Hospital and the Philadelphia Divinity School. This last institution also owes its beginnings to the Civil War which made it difficult for northern boys to go to Alexandria for training.

In 1858, he was given relief by the election of the Reverend Samuel Bowman, Rector of St. James, Lancaster, as his assistant. Bishop Bowman died three years later on a journey into the western part of the Diocese and he was succeeded by the Reverend William B. Stevens. After 1860, much of the burden of the Diocese fell upon the assistants, for Bishop Potter suffered two strokes of paralysis from which he never completely recovered. In 1865, he set out with his third wife for a honeymoon voyage to California. At the first port of call in Peru he received the news of Lincoln's assassination, and, like the rest of the North, was greatly saddened by the tragedy. He must have felt particularly close to the Lincoln administration since the Secretary of State was his old friend and fellow student at Union, William H. Seward. He was ill with "Panama fever" when they docked in San Francisco and he died on the ship July 4, 1865. He was held in such esteem three thousand miles from home that a committee of clergy and laity accompanied the body on the voyage back to New York.

Bishop Stevens succeeded to the Diocese. In the following year, the western third was erected into the Diocese of Pittsburgh and in 1871 Central Pennsylvania was set apart as the third Diocese in the state.

Such was the nature and background of the Diocese to which Bishop Darlington journeyed after his Consecration.

Chapter Three

IN THE DAYS OF BISHOP DARLINGTON

I

The cordial reception which Bishop Darlington received on his arrival in Harrisburg was typical of those he was to receive in the parishes and missions as he made his visitations. Before coming to Harrisburg, he had asked Mr. Morrison, President of the Standing Committee, to arrange an itinerary which would enable him to get some impression of his Diocese before Convention in June. In seven weeks, he had visited twenty-eight parishes and missions, in twelve of which he had had Confirmations, and he had been in every part of the Diocese. During the first year, he visited every parish, organized mission and mission station at least once and in some instances, several times. During these visits, he was constantly on the alert to seek out new opportunities to extend the work of the Church. In his early Convention addresses, he never failed to express his pleasure and appreciation for the hearty manner in which he was received everywhere he went. The following quotation from the address to the Convention of 1910 will illustrate his attitude:

"Being born in New York City and having spent nearly all my life there, it was to be expected that I would make mistakes, and, for a time at least, feel somewhat unaccustomed with conditions in a Diocese so largely rural. The cordial hospitality of all the men and women of the Diocese, soon made me feel at home. It seems to me today, almost as though I had not lived anywhere else. Not alone the members of our own Church, but all citizens of the State; Jewish and Christian, Roman and Protestant, Greek and Quaker— as well as the members of our own Catholic communion have been more than kind, and helped me in many ways while on my constant travels through the State. County and State officials, railroad officers and employees, newspaper editors, school teachers, hotel proprietors and traveling men have been most obliging. In this public way, I take the present occasion to thank all these whom I can repay in no other way than by this grateful acknowledgement of their courtesy."

This may have been, as the Bishop said in another address, a manifestation of our Pennsylvania hospitality, but it was as surely a response to the warmth of his personality. He encouraged his clergy and laity to visit him at his residences in Harrisburg and Williamsport; he showed a sympathetic understanding of the problems confronting parish and mission: his words were words of courage and inspiration; his outlook was forward looking and optimistic.

He travelled incessantly to make himself available for functions that were of special interest to his people. Nor did he confine his energies to matters immediately connected with his Diocese. He took an active part in civic enterprises; he counselled with other Protestant bodies; he was Chairman of the State Sunday School Convention when it met in Harrisburg in 1910; he was deeply interested in the Men and Religion Forward Movement; and he maintained a close relation with the various Orthodox Churches within the bounds of the Diocese. When he was called to speak outside the Diocese—and there were so many such engagements that the wits referred to him as "the Bishop *from* Harrisburg"—whenever possible he took occasion to present the needs and problems of his Diocese; from Rhode Island to Florida he called the Church to a realization of its duty to the coal miners with whose plight he was especially sympathetic.

Wherever he went, his common sense, his scholarship, his understanding and his optimism won for him love and respect. The Diocese knew that it had for its leader a true Father-in-God. Coldspring cannot congeal the warmth of his spirit. For example, consider how, like a benediction, these words must have fallen on the ears of the missionary living in isolation and discouraged that he was making so little progress:

> "Do not be discouraged if the growth in your own field of labor be not as great as some other parish can report. Despise not the day of small things. There is a time for sowing and a time for reaping. Both he that sows and he that reaps are equally God's faithful husbandmen. Both have their place in the church, and are equally necessary. It is weary waiting sometimes, but the promise is 'ye shall reap if ye faint not'. It may be that Rector, Vestry and faithful women have given their prayers, their time, their

(34)

best thought, and their hard earned money—yet the increase of Church and Sunday School seems very slow and not what had been so earnestly hoped for. Perhaps, dear Christian workers and brethren, God is trying your faith for a time. Perhaps He is even now waiting 'to be gracious', and give you soon that outpouring of His Holy Spirit, which will convert the indifferent and convict the gainsayers."

In his address to the Convention which had met to celebrate the tenth anniversary of the setting apart of the Diocese, Bishop Darlington's personality seems to come alive as he spoke to the assembled delegates. We quote him at length not only that we of this generation may catch something of the spirit of our first Bishop, but because the words have a message as much for our day as for his:

"Thankfulness is only thinkfulness, and caused by reflection on the Almighty's longsuffering and patience with His people in the past. Our part is to show that we appreciate our blessings, and to be more unselfish and prayerful hereafter. As Frederick Morris never read a book without a prayer, so may we begin and finish each day's pleasure or task with the same. Make God your Director.

"Under His direction, in the words of the familiar Collect, we will have 'most gracious favor and continual help' when 'all our works' are 'begun, continued and ended' in Him. If we are not answered, it will be because Omniscience and Love refuse permission to harm ourselves or others, or because we have, by our sins, severed the connection and relation established by faith.

"God will force no man's will. If we choose to abide in the dark abodes of wickedness, and shut out the light: or if we, merely through defiant indifference, walk by deliberate choice on the cold, shady side of the street, the warm beams of His sunshine will never find us, but the moment we care enough for ourselves or others to come out of our darkness and coldness and change our places, seek the brightness of the Sun of Righteousness, we will find awaiting us the health, happiness and strength which might have been ours long ago had we sought it.

(35)

"The sun ever shines down into the world's gloom from the throne of God in that land where no night is, and only they lose it, who willfully refuse to see. 'Open thy mouth wide, and I will fill it', are God's words. His mercy is over all His works. He promises that He may reward. He threatens that He may not punish. Haeckel may compare all processes to the formation of a crystal, but the conversion of an immortal spirit from rebellion to childlike submission has no parallel in the material laws or processes. I believe in material laws for material objects, and in spiritual laws for spiritual growth. These laws are equally true, but they are not the same. This world is bound by silken, not iron chains to the feet of God.

"Prayer is the overruler and conqueror of all spiritual and material substances and states. Faith gives to feeble men the power of giants to cast out devils, and through Christ abolished fleshly lusts and death. 'This is the victory that overcometh the world, even our faith', writes St. John. 'If we are to live at all, we must live, and civilization can only live, by religion', says Professor Seely of Cambridge: and William James writes, 'There is only one unconditional commandment, which is that we should seek incessantly with fear and trembling, so to vote and act as to bring about the very largest total universe of good which we can see.'

"Seek to Know thyself and find by prayer the work of God meant for you to do. Each one was created for a special task, and it will be forever undone unless we find it and perform it."

During his long Rectorship in Brooklyn, Bishop Darlington made important connections which he did not sever on coming to the Diocese. He was constantly being called back to marry the young people he had brought in to the Church as children. His Christmas sermons were a tradition at Christ Church. It was to New York and his old Diocese of Long Island that he went to recruit the clergy to fill his vacancies. As far as possible, he kept his interest in the cultural organizations to which he had formerly belonged. He had an independent income, so that he could afford to spent his summers at Newport, Rhode Island. He literally "walked with kings" when

(36)

he visited Europe during the summer of 1908 to attend the Lambeth Conference. But wherever he went, the Diocese was always close to his heart and he used his connections to enhance its prestige and to strengthen its personnel.

As might be expected of a Bishop, he was called upon to play his part in directing the affairs of the National Church. One project in which he was especially interested was his work with the Committee to prepare a Mission Hymnal. Because of his love for music, he was eminently fitted to take part in this important task. Thus, this young Diocese became widely known throughout the Church since it had for its Bishop the Right Reverend James Henry Darlington.

There are evidences in the early Journals of the Diocese which reveal that the first decade of the twentieth century would have been unfamiliar territory to the modern Churchman. For one thing, the Sunday evening service was as much a part of the parish program as the eleven o'clock service (more often than not held at 10:30) and often more largely attended. This made it possible for the missionary with two or more stations to minister effectively to large congregations. Sunday afternoon was generally accepted as the proper time for holding Sunday School; to suggest getting little children out in the early morning, especially in winter, was almost sadistic. It was quite possible, too, to gather a congregation on a week night.

The Bishop did not hesitate to schedule Confirmations during the week and, in some instances, even on a Saturday night. August had not become generally recognized as the vacation month. If a parson got any vacation at all, except in very rare cases, it was a short one. That these were "horse and buggy days" was brought out in Archdeacon McMillan's report to the Convention of 1915. Commenting on the purchase of an automobile by the Reverend William Dorwart so that he might the more easily make the trip between Newport, Thompsontown, and Millersburg, he said, "The automobile has been of great assistance. It can be said to have passed the experimental stage. in efficiency and economy it has justified the venture."

In those days, only a select few attended the public High School, and those who did engaged in few extracurricular activities. Public

Youth centers and recreational programs were twenty years in the future. Scouts and kindred organizations were in their infancy. Yet, the problem of an increased leisure became a matter of concern to the Church. The Girls' Friendly and The Daughters of the King partially met the needs of the girls, but it was evident that something must be done to supply the social needs of the teenagers of both sexes. Young priests coming out of the seminary were eager to tackle this problem. Through their enthusiasm, parish houses were built in many places often equipped with gymnasiums, and auditoriums. They organized boys' clubs, craft clubs, and men's clubs. To meet the needs of the older young people, night classes in sewing, stenography and homemaking were often formed.

In meeting this leisure time problem, the Episcopal Church was in a strategic position since it did not frown on dancing and card playing as did many of the other churches in Central Pennsylvania in that day. Thus, through its social program, many came into contact with the Church, and were later brought into the Church by Confirmation.

The choir also served to bring many into the Church. Since most Protestant churches frowned on vestments and none had Junior choirs, it was comparatively easy to get boys for the choir. Parents were glad to have their boys get the musical training and the boys loved the vestments and processions. It is not surprising to learn then, that even the smaller parishes reported having large choirs. Listening every Sunday to the noble words of the Prayer Book, and taking part in the orderly dignified service, many boys became candidates for Confirmation and through them their parents were brought into the Church. Many priests assert that they first became interested in the Church through the choir.

In spite of the influence of the parish house and the choir in adding numbers to the Church, the growth of the Church in the Diocese was discouragingly slow. Central Pennsylvania was not "Episcopal Country". The clergy found a resistance to the Church which they felt was born of prejudice and misunderstanding. In some cases churches had been built by patrons in communities where there was a considerable English population and the impression prevailed in these communities that the church was exclusive and that others were not welcome. As a result, these churches were hard put

(38)

to it to survive when the patron withdrew his support and economic conditions caused a shift in population. But the real obstacle to growth was a prejudice against the Episcopal Church which often became vocal in the phrase "They are next door to the Catholics." It was the opinion of some of our clergy that this prejudice was being fostered by some of the school histories then in current use. Accordingly, in 1909, a committee composed of the Rev. Messrs. Houghton, Doggles and Quinn and Mr. Richard M. H. Wharton was appointed to examine school text books and report to the Convention of 1910. The findings made interesting reading. Because the information is still timely after forty years, we feel justified in quoting at length from the report:

"From a careful examination of their works, we find that they teach:—

"1. That a new Church was founded in England in the 16th century.

"2. That the Tudor monarchs made themselves spiritual and moral as well as civil and political heads of the Church, i. e. they made themselves heads of the Church in the same sense as the Pope was of the Roman Church and as if they claimed and exercised Episcopal and sacerdotal functions.

"3. That the Creeds were changed and new Creeds formulated.

"4. Though not stated in so many words, the definite impression is given that the substitution of the English Book of Common Prayer for the Latin services involved an absolute break in the continuity of worship and in the administration of the Sacraments.

"5. That Church Property before the Reformation was Roman Catholic Church Property, that it was seized or stolen and became the property of the State and Church of England.

"6. The title "Catholic" is invariably used for Roman Catholics only. One general assumption running through all the work of all of these writers when treating of this period, is that submission to the Papacy constitutes Catholicism and that there are no Catholics but Roman Catholics. Another assumption pervading their works is that the Eng-

(39)

lish Reformation was carried out on the same principles and produced the same results as the Continental Reformation; that is, it was a Revolution.

"7. That grossly exaggerated credit is given to the Puritans and New England in promoting religious freedom and political liberty while comparatively little credit is given to Virginia, and the Church of England is disparaged and belittled. Finally the authorities used and quoted are either literary stylists like McCauley and Froude, reputed infidels as Hume and Meyers or enemies and outsiders as Gasquet and Fisher, while our own are ignored or given second or even third place."

While these authors have been displaced by others in our public school history courses, the general impression remains about the same. The report sums up the results of this kind of teaching in these words:

1. "That many of the children of the Church and many of their elders also have the idea that the English Church with her American and Colonial daughters—the whole Anglican Communion—is but one of the older, more dignified and liturgical offspring of Martin Luther; that it was organized by a vicious Bluebeard named Henry the Eighth whose work was completed by his illegitimate children, and that what religion we have, in addition to what the Bible and the Reformers gave us, comes to us through a first Church known as the Roman Catholic.

2. That many of our children and people who are better instructed are sadly perplexed by the conflict of authority between the Church's teaching on the one hand and that of the schools and many popular historians on the other They say, 'You' say so and so but History teaches Such and such.

3. No wonder then that our clergy and our customs, worship and institutions have become the common sport and plaything of many popular novelists from George Elliot and Mrs. Humphrey Ward to Hall Cain and Marie Correlli.

. . . .

5. The multitudes of immigrants and their children longing for privileges of Catholicism and weary of the op-

pression of Romanism are deterred and withheld from finding their true home in that Catholic Body which we love to call the American Church."

Despite difficulties, the Church sought to open up new fields. It was inspired to this end by Bishop Darlington, Mr. Baker, the General Missionary and the Archdeacons. The missionary priests, often working under most trying conditions and at starvation wages, were anxious to establish the Church wherever opportunity offered. The Diocese was kept missionary-minded by having to listen to reports of the state of its missions every year at Convention. Again and again, the Board of Missions pleaded for more adequate support and, had it been forthcoming, the Church in many communities in the Diocese would have been in a stronger position today. Discouraged by the frequent changes in the leadership and by the long intervals without services of a priest Church families were often drawn away to other communions. Yet the list of places where new work was begun between 1905 and 1915 is quite impressive.

In Harrisburg, St. Augustine's Mission was opened to serve the colored population, and a similar work was established at St. Barnabas' Mission in Altoona. In the older part of the Diocese, work was started at Elizabethtown and Quarryville in Lancaster County; at Hanover in York County, Mount Alto in the southern part of the Cumberland Valley and at Camp Hill and New Market in the Northern End.

Mr. Dorwart, missionary at Newport, at various times, had preaching stations at Duncannon, Millerstown, Loysville, Port Royal and Mifflintown. He even extended his operation across the Susquehanna to Millersburg where he organized St. Bartholomew's.

In the coal regions, Ascension, Kulpmont and St. George's, Coal Run were organized; and across the river from Danville Grace Church, Riverside, began operations. Along the West Branch of the Susquehanna, missions were established at South Williamsport, Halls, Dewart and Watsontown.

In the western end of the Diocese, there was a preaching at Mount Union, a mission at Everett, and two missions in the Altoona area—St. Peter's, Juniata, and Holy Trinity, Hollidaysburg. In the Northern Tier, new missions were opened at Nordmont, Lawrenceville, Galeton, Ulysses and Austin.

One of the most far-sighted pieces of missionary work undertaken during this period was the opening of St. Andrew's, State College, believed to be the first mission church, which was designed to serve college students in the United States, cooperatively financed by several dioceses. On the urging of the Rev. John Hewitt of Bellefonte, Bishop Darlington became greatly interested in this new work, and enlisted the cooperation of all five dioceses of Pennsylvania. The Rev. Edward M. Frear began a long career there in January, 1911, as the first chaplain to Episcopal students at Penn State. With the aid of many loyal helpers, he carried an appeal for funds to all dioceses of the state. During the diocesan convention held at St. John's, Bellefonte, in May, 1911, ground was broken for the first small church at State College.

As a further evidence of advance, St. Andrew's, Harrisburg, and Trinity, Tyrone, changed their status from organized missions to incorporated parishes. On the other hand, the work at St. David's, Delta; Incarnation, York; St. George's, Hanover; St. James, Greencastle and some of the smaller preaching stations had to be abandoned.

To assist the struggling churches, Bishop Darlington organized what he called "The Bishop's Hand." This was an organization of men who agreed to respond to not more than five calls a year by contributing at least one dollar. It was not the custom to make Sunday to Sunday contributions to what we now call the Field Work Fund, but the Missionary Society of the Diocese was supported by special collections. Toward the end of the period, an effort was made to train the people in the use of duplex envelop, and as the practice became more general the work of the Missionary Society was put on a sounder basis. The Diocese found it difficult in the early days to meet even the budget for current expenses. For example, in 1906 the Convention took up a special collection among the delegates to meet the current deficit of $500.00.

Not only was the Bishop anxious to see the Church grow in numbers, but he was deeply concerned about the nurture of the children. It was the general understanding that Sunday School completely covered the field of Christian Education. The Diocesan Board of Education operated on an annual budget of about $50.00 and it received little help from the National Church. Indeed the Budget of the National Church for Christian education did not exceed

(42)

$30,000.00. To improve the standard of teaching and to inspire teachers to realize the importance of their task, the Sunday School Committee arranged for teachers' institutes to be conducted on a Diocesan basis. The first of these was held at the Yeates School, September 21-22, 1911. The Committee was disappointed in the response, since only those from the Lancaster area found it possible to attend. After a second attempt in 1912, with no better result, the project was abandoned in favor of regional institutes.

In 1906 the Bishop appointed a committee with the Reverend William F. Shero as Chairman to prepare a Sunday School Curriculum which could be used throughout the Diocese. Their recommendations make interesting reading:

First, Second and Third Years: Bible stories from Old and New Testament. Oral teaching with pictures. Instruction on practical and religious duties. Memorizing suitable prayers, hymns and texts.

Fourth Year: Elementary study of the Church Catechism, and the Christian Year.

Fifth Year: New Testament lessons illustrating the Church Catechism.

Sixth Year: Old Testament lessons illustrating the Church Catechism.

Seventh Year: Study of the Church Catechism.

Eighth Year—First Half: Study of the Prayer Book. Second Half: Introduction to the Bible.

Ninth Year: Study of the Collects, Epistle and Gospels.

Tenth Year: Study of the Old Testament preparation for Christ.

Eleventh Year: Study of the Life of Our Lord.

Twelfth Year: Study of the Acts and Epistles.

The Social Service Committee devoted its labors chiefly to drawing the attention of the Diocese in its annual reports to the evils of child labor and the liquor traffic. The country seemed to be moving steadily toward "Prohibition." Bishop Darlington was much interested in this movement, and he preached temperance in season and out. An interesting note in his diary tells how he induced a man "to sign the pledge" while they were waiting for the midnight train at Muncy.

With the passing years, came changes in leadership. After serving a year, Mr. Freeze resigned as Chancellor and was succeeded by Mr. C. LaRue Munson of Williamsport; Mr. Alricks, the treasurer, died in 1913, and his place was taken by Mr. Herbert W. Hartman of Lancaster. Except at St. Stephen's, Harrisburg, all the larger churches had a change of leadership. In Lancaster Dr. Breed, was succeeded at St. James by the Reverend Clifford G. Twombly, and at St. John's, Dr. Shero was succeeded by the Reverend George Israel Browne; the Reverend Arthur H. Taylor succeeded the Reverend Charles Wood at St. John's, York; Mr. Morrison was followed at Sunbury by the Reverend Walter C. Pugh; Mr. Diggles, at Bloomsburg by the Reverend Frederick O. Musser; in Williamsport, Dr. Foley was succeeded at Trinity by the Reverend Robert F. Gibson, and Mr. Eckel at Christ Church, by the Reverend W. Northy Jones; Dr. Clerc at Philipsburg was succeeded by the Reverend Franklin T. Eastmant, and at Altoona, the Reverend Allen Sheldon Woodle finished a long Rectorship and his place was taken by the Reverend George R. Bishop.

In an attempt to create Diocesan consciousness, the annual Convention was held in churches in all parts of the Diocese. Between 1905 and 1915, the following churches entertained the Convention: St. Stephen's, Harrisburg; Christ Church, Williamsport; St. Matthew's, Sunbury; St. Paul's, Lock Haven; Trinity, Shamokin; St. Luke's, Altoona; St. John's, Bellefonte; St. John's, York; St. Paul's, Bloomsburg; St. James, Lancaster. In 1915, Convention returned to St. Stephen's, Harrisburg, where the Bishop celebrated his tenth anniversary. The business at these conventions was largely routine. Three matters deserve mention in passing. In 1907, the Diocese adopted its present seal. For those interested in heraldry, the following resolution introduced by a Committee in the Convention of 1907 will be interesting:

The seal shall contain the arms of the Diocese of Harrisburg which are established as follows: *Or,* on a Celtic Cross *sable—A DOVE DESCENDING ARGENT;* on a chief of the second, between a crescent of the third (for Harris) and a plate (for Penn) a rose of the third enclosed in another gules spined proper (for Lancaster and York); above the shield the legend "SEAL OF THE DIOCESE OF HARRISBURG." The shield enclosed in a vesica.

(44)

The motto of the Diocese shall be Spiritu Dum Spiro Spero. (In the Spirit while I breathe I hope.)

The Plan of having two See Cities soon proved unsatisfactory. n 1909, the Bishop gave up the idea of summering in Williamsport nd the Standing Committee purchased an Episcopal Residence at 321 Jorth Front Street, Harrisburg, which served in this capacity until 943. Overlooking the park and the river, it was then in the best eighborhood in the city, for in the first decade of this century the lite of Harrisburg had mansions on Front Street, Walnut and State. t was but a few doors away from the Governor's Mansion with hich it compared favorably in size and appointments. On the first oor was the formal reception room, the beautiful Keferstein Me-iorial Chapel of the Holy Spirit, and what amounted to a state din-ig room. On the second floor was the Bishop's study and a large Baronial Hall" where assemblies of considerable size could gather, vhere distinguished visitors were entertained, and where St. Steph-n's choir came to sing carols at Christmas time. It was in keeping rith the standards of gracious living of the Victorian period and in ie tradition of the palaces of the English Bishops and was appropri-tely named "Bishopscourt."

Finally, Convention realigned the Archdeaconries. The Arch-eaconry of Altoona included the churches in Blair, Huntingdon, Jifflin, Juniata, Fulton and Bedford Counties., and Philipsburg in entre County; the Archdeaconry of Harrisburg included the coun-ies of Perry, Dauphin, Lancaster, York, Adams and Franklin. The est of the Diocese was the Archdeaconry of Williamsport. The Reverend Franklin T. Eastmant was Archdeacon of Altoona, the Reverend Alexander McMillan, Archdeacon of Harrisburg, and the Reverend Lewis Nichols, Archdeacon of Williamsport.

II

The quiet routine of American life was rudely interrupted in the ummer of 1914. On the morning of June 29, the American people ead in their newspapers that the Archduke of Austria had been assas-inated the day before by a Serbian student in the city of Sarajevo. Jone in this country suspected that this was the match that would et off the powder keg which was western Europe. The terms im-

(45)

posed by Austria upon Serbia were so harsh that she felt she could not accept them and maintain her self respect, and assured of the support of Russia, she rejected them summarily. With Russia allied with Serbia, Germany came to Austria's defense according to the terms of the Triple Alliance. Then France entered on the side of Russia. While England had entered into a friendly understanding with France and Russia, her position did not become clear until Germany violated Belgian neutrality in order to make a quick disposition of France before the Russian Bear could shake himself awake.

The secret diplomacy which caused this explosion was unknown to most Americans. It was simply a matter of academic interest to others. But American emotions were deeply stirred by the news of German cruelty in Belgium, by the gallant defense of Liege, by the relentless progress of the German war machine into France and the stubborn stand of the French forces at the Marne which saved Paris a repetition of the experience of being occupied by a enemy nation.

At the outbreak of the war, President Wilson issued the usual proclamation of neutrality but he also urged the American people to remain neutral in their sympathy. This seemed easy enough since the causes of the war seemed very confused and the issue not well defined. Furthermore, it seemed that the only part we could play was that of interested spectators whose good offices as mediator might be of value at war's end. It was not long, however, till it was brought forcibly to our attention that we could not hope to continue our normal course of life unaffected by the upheaval in Europe. As a neutral nation, we had contended for a century that we enjoyed the freedom of the sea. As in the days before the War of 1812, this right was now challenged by Great Britain who stopped our ships and searched them for contraband. American indignation was aroused by this unwarranted interference with our rights and was fanned into flame by schoolboy memories of George III and the Irish-Americans who regarded Great Britain as the source of all the misery which their native land was suffering. It was all that Ambassador Page could do to avoid an open break and he might not have succeeded had not Germany committed greater injury.

With her fleet bottled up in the Kiehl Canal, Germany realized that Great Britain, being "Mistress of the Seas" could speedily bring her to her knees through starvation. Her only defense against the flow of American goods to the Allies was the submarine or U-boat. To be effective, this little craft had to strike without warning, and, of course, no provision could be made for the safety of the passengers and crew of the torpedoed shhip. What all this could mean came home to us in America on May 7, 1915, when the great liner *Lusitania* was sunk without warning off the Irish coast with the loss of more than eleven hundred lives, one hundred twenty-four of whom were American citizens. The country cried out for action, but the President counselled patience. For the next year and a half he sought, by diplomatic pressure, to get Germany to abandon this ruthless policy. During the exchange of notes, American sentiment veered more and more to the side of the Allies as it bcame clearer that the issue of the war was Democracy vs. Tyranny. Still, our people were reluctant to enter actively into the struggle, preferring to support the Allied cause with goods and money. When, in 1916, Germany agreed to stop her indiscriminate submarine warfare, it appeared that Wilson's policy had paid off, and he won a close election on the basis that he had kept us out of war.

Conditions changed radically after the new year with Germany's announcement that she would resume unrestricted submarine warfare. During the winter, it became increasingly evident that we could no longer remain neutral and in a historic speech before a joint session of Congress on April 2, President Wilson asked for a Declaration of War upon the Imperial German government. Four days later, Congress granted his request by an overwhelming vote and, for the first time in half a century we were in a major conflict.

America entered the war in the spirit of a crusader. Coveting no territory and with no selfish aims, the nation girded itself to make the world safe for democracy. The National Guard, fresh from active duty on the Mexican border, was quickly inducted into Federal service and sent off to training camp. In June, General Pershing landed in France with a small force as concrete evidence that we meant to take an active part in the war. Young men from all walks of life volunteered their services and the Selective Service Act brought the more reluctant into the conflict. The Salvation Army, the Red Cross and the Y. M. C. A. leaped into popularity because of their war work and their drives for funds met generous response as did the four calls by the government for the purchase of Liberty Bonds.

By the spring of 1918, a constant stream of soldiers converged upon New York to be ferried across the Atlantic thence to take their place in American divisions which at Chateau Thierry and the Argonne checked the advance of the great German offensive. We had not begun to reach our war potential when the Central Powers began to collapse and the news reached us that Germany had signed an armistice on November 11, that the Kaiser had abdicated and Germany would be a Republic. It looked as though the only barrier to freedom had been battered down, and as America prepared to spend a joyous and peaceful Christmas, it seemed that the angels' promise of peace on earth was about to be fulfilled.

Such momentous events could not but leave their stamp upon the Diocese of Harrisburg. Having our roots in England, the Episcopal Church found it easier to see the justice of the Allied cause than did churches in Pennsylvania which had a German origin. Bishop Darlington had strong sympathy for France. But no official notice was taken of the war until the United States had committed itself. The convention which met a month after the declaration of war expressed the mind of the Diocese in the following resolution:

BE IT RESOLVED:

That at this first annual convention of the Diocese of Harrisburg after the Declaration of War, the Bishop Clergy and Lay delegates desire to put themselves on record.

FIRST, That we are ready and desirous to sustain in every way in our power, the President of the United States, and the Senate and House of Representatives in Congress assembled in the immediate and efficient completion of their military and naval preparations;

SECOND, That we unanimously deem this conflict into which with no selfish aim on our part for increase of territory or any material advantage we have been reluctantly forced as the Defense of Democracy against Despotism and a Confederacy of Christianity and Civilization against Military Cruelty in which present war is the price which must be paid for permanent peace;

THIRD, That we are grateful and proud that many of German descent and bearing honored German names are the most loyal, devoted and generous supporters of the United

(48)

States in this time of stress,

FOURTH, That we urge each Rector and vestry, where it has not already been done, to see that the National Flag is shown in each Church, and that the special prayers authorized by our Diocesan be used at all services till the war's end.

In addition to authorizing the special prayers referred to in the resolution Bishop Darlington commended the use of the Star Spangled Banner and the Battle Hymn of the Republic—hymns not included in the Hymnal in 1892 which was then in general use.

The next convention met in Lock Haven just before the great summer offensive got under way. It is not surprising that the spirit of the gathering was patriotic. Breaking a long standing precedent, Convention opened at four in the afternoon instead of seven-thirty in the evening in order that the evening might be given over to a great War Dinner held at the State Teachers' College at which distinguished representatives of France and Canada were present and spoke. The feature of the afternoon service was the presentation to St. Paul's parish of the flags of several of the Allied Nations, which flags were to be a permanent possession of the church. The choir of St. Paul's sang the National Anthem of each of the countries whose flags the Bishop blessed. The account of this service, printed in the Journal of 1918, reflects the mood of the time:

In the solemn processional at the opening service of the Convention the flags of the Allied Nations of the United States, Great Britain, France and Italy were borne by the following color bearers: Edgar F. Heffner, Jr., Harrison T. Beardsley, 3rd, Thomas F. Heffner and Melvin Kepler.

Evening Prayer being ended, the color bearers carried their several flags down the main aisle of the Church and returned escorting with them the sponsors for the respective flags.

At the chancel rail Major General Charles M. Clement, National Army, retired, presented to the Bishop the United States flag; the Bishop having taken it from his hands signed it with the sign of the cross and offered the following invocation:

"Oh God of our Fathers; bless this emblem of our country, the United States of America; and make us worthy of

(49)

it. May the red of Christ's blood, the white purity of thy spirit, and the blue of God's firmament symbolize to us things sacred as well as patriotic; that we render to the nation the loyalty due earthly governance and to Heaven the things of heaven. As one star differeth from another star in glory: so give our army and navy a happy life or a glorious passing to paradise and save them and us from our baser selves and sinning. (Here the Bishop made the sign of the cross.) We ask it all through the Captain of our salvation Jesus Christ, our Lord. Amen."

Sir John Willison of the Dominion of Canada then presented to the Bishop the Union Jack of Great Britain; the Bishop having taken it from his hands signed it with the sign of the cross and offered the following prayer of benediction:

"Lord God of truth and righteousness; we ask Thy blessing upon this flag of England. May the Motherland in her island home and her children all over the round world be united in ties based upon kindred blood; but kept strong by ever-increasing respect and mutual appreciation of each other's love for Righteousness, Justice and Truth. May differences in the past be forgotten and the United States and England be hereafter 'one and inseparable' for the world's freedom and peace forever; (here the Bishop made the sign of the cross) through Jesus Christ our Lord. Amen."

M. Stephane Lauzanne of the French Mission to the United States, then presented to the Bishop the Tricolor Flag of France; the Bishop having taken it from his hands signed it with the sign of the cross and offered the following prayer of benediction:

"Oh God of battles as well as of peace: bless this unconquerable emblem of the French Nation that through the self-sacrifice of so many hundred thousands of her noble sons which she has been called to bear, she may attain a glory and consecration nationally never known before. May our two sister republics be ever bound together by deepest admiration and love, ready as in the past to afford instant help in time of stress and life, Jeanne d'Arc seeing visions of future

(50)

service for God and Humanity, which through prayer and patriotism we may have strength to carry out. (Here the Bishop made the sign of the cross) through Jesus Christ our Lord. Amen."

William Caprio of Lock Haven, a native of Italy, then presented to the Bishop the Italian flag; the Bishop having taken it from his hands signed it with the sign of the cross and offered the following prayer of benediction:

"Oh God of the mighty past and of the still greater present and future; we ask thy blessing on the land, the army and the people of this devoted country. May the liberty of thought and conscience now theirs enable one and all to strive to regain their ancient world leadership in Art, in Music and in Literature, that Italy may bless all lands by her devotion to personal freedom, brotherly love and justice, (here the Bishop made the sign of the cross) through Jesus Christ our Lord. Amen."

The respective sponsors then returned to their places in the church and the Bishop proceeded with the final collects and then dismissed the congregation with his blessing.

The Convention of 1919 met while the Peace Conference was in progress in Paris. This excerpt from the Bishop's address to that convention reflects not only his feelings but much of the temper of the time:

It was my privilege at the Provincial Synod of Washington to propose and advocate three resolutions which were passed unanimously. If they meet your approval, I would be gratified to have such resolutions carried here for the consideration of the Peace Conference. The first, that we request the Cathedral Church of San Sophia in Constantinople, now called the Mosque of Mar, be returned to Orthodox Christian worship, that this historic center of Christian worship shall become "a house of prayer for all people."

Second, that if possible the treaty of peace when finally adopted shall be called the peace of Jerusalem, to fulfill the old prophecies which speak of the "law going forth from Mount Zion" and of Jerusalem as "the joy of the whole earth." The name Jerusalem means peace, and nearby is

(51)

Bethlehem where the Prince of Peace was born, and where the angels sang, "Peace on earth, good will to men."

Third, That as sermons generally are introduced by a prayer to God and men's last testaments or wills begin with the words, "In the Name of God: Amen," so this solemn and momentous expression of the opinion of the civilized world that war should cease forever, should also begin by invoking the name of the Almighty God and His blessing on all that follows."

But it was not the passage of resolutions, the holding of special services, nor the singing of patriotic hymns in church that brought the war home to the people of the Diocese. In every community young men were exchanging their civilian clothes for the uniform of their country, and crowds gathered at the railroad stations to bid a solemn farewell to those who were destined for the training camp. For these men, the war meant the complete severance of home ties, for no provision was made to take their families to training camp and furloughs were infrequent.

When a soldier left his training camp, it was a common experience for him not to return till he had received his discharge. The service flags which were placed in our churches and dedicated by Bishop Darlington during the winter of 1917-1918 testified to the number of Episcopal homes in which the war had a very personal meaning.

Moreover, at least three training centers were located within the bounds of the Diocese. A large cantonment was located on the old battlefield at Gettysburg where the Reverend Charles S. Kitchin served as Chaplain to the Tank Corps; a camp for negroes was located at March Run along the Susquehanna where the Reverend Willoughby M. Parchment acted as part-time Chaplain in connection with his duties as Vicar of the Church of the Holy Cross at Harrisburg; at the Aviation camp at Middletown, Dr. Appleton combined his duties as Rector of St. Paul's, Harrisburg, with a part-time Chaplaincy. The Reverend George T. LaScelle and the Reverend Frederick O. Musser went to Chaplains' Training School but the Armistice was signed by the time they completed their training and both preferred to return to their parishes rather than continue in military service.

The war produced a considerable dislocation of population in many Diocesan communities. Everywhere the loss of young men was keenly felt in the church. High wages in war plants lured many from their former homes. Many communities (particularly in Tioga County) found their economic base cut from under them. Moreover, when the war was over many of these young men never returned to their former homes, preferring the opportunities of city life for those in the country. The author of the popular song then current in the nation was prophet as well as poet when he raised the question, "How're you goin' to keep 'em down on the farm after they've seen Paree?"

Though not so dramatic, the war had yet another serious effect upon the Diocese of Harrisburg. During the years 1915-20, prices rose sharply. Assigning the number 100 as the price index of 1913, the index number for the year 1920 was 226. As usual, in inflation periods, wages lagged behind prices. This situation was surely reflected in contributions to the church and more seriously reflected in the salaries the clergy received. In order for a clergyman not to be working for reduced wages his 1920 salary would need to be more than double his salary for 1913. In no instance was this true. A comparison of the salaries of some of our clergy for the years 1913 and 1920 will reveal the salary scale and also the suffering the current inflation must have cost them:

A SELECTED LIST OF CLERICAL SALARIES

Place	1913	1920
Altoona: St. Luke's	$1,500	$2,400
Bellefonte	1,300	1,500
Bloomsburg	1,200	1,800
Carlisle	1,400	1,800
Chambersburg	825	1,400
Columbia	1,000	1,400
Danville	1,200	1,200
Harrisburg:		
St. Andrew's	800	1,500
St. Paul's	1,500	1,400
St. Stephen's	2,018	3,000
Huntingdon	840	1,200

Lancaster:

St. James	2,600	4,000
St. John's	1,730	2,100
Lewistown	1,000	1,500
Lock Haven	1,283	1,800
Philipsburg	1,200	1,800
Shamokin	1,000	1,200
Sunbury	1,500	2,100
Tyrone	600	1,380
Wellsboro	1,200	1,400
Williamsport:		
Christ	3,649	3,750
Trinity	1,800	3,600
York: St. John's	3,720	3,600

While the war was drawing to its end in the fall of 1918, an epidemic of Spanish influenza was visited upon the nation. Striking first at the army camps, it quickly spread throughout the land leaving panic and death in its wake. The nature of the disease was unknown and the doctors were virtually helpless to cope with it. It was believed that there was special danger of people gathered in crowds, so the state of Pennsylvania imposed a general quarantine from September 27 to November 11. During this period, all public gatherings were banned in the state. This, of course, had its effect upon the church. While central Pennsylvania did not suffer as greatly as did the great cities of Philadelphia and Pittsburgh, nevertheless, the list of deaths which the Bishop noted in his address of 1919 was unusually long. It is significant that while the churches were closed for six weeks, no serious effect is registered in their influence.

In 1919, the requisite number of states ratified the Eighteenth Amendment to the Constitution providing for nationwide prohibition. While not scheduled to take effect before January 16, 1920, it was put in force almost immediately after its passage as a war measure to conserve grain. The proposal to ban the sale of alcoholic liquor did not seem at all drastic in those days. Sentiment in that direction had been growing steadily and by the time the war broke out one-half of the population was living in "dry" territory. The Diocese of Harrisburg, being so largely rural, had exiled the saloon in many of its counties by local option. The Bishop was an ardent advocate of temperance; the Social Service Committee had devoted one of its reports to the evils of the liquor traffic; Convention had passed a resolution urging the State Legislature to ratify the amendment; and it was the consensus of opinion that Prohibition was a move in the right direction and that the experiment would succeed. Convention recommended to the people of the Diocese that they cheerfully comply with the law, but a resolution recommending the use of unfermented grape juice in celebrating the Holy Communion was defeated.

The Suffrage Movement which culminated in the passage of the 19th Amendment was reflected in the councils of the Diocese by a discussion of the propriety of women holding Church office. The Bishop expressed the opinion that he has no objection to this, but he preferred that women did not sit on vestries or hold such positions as Church Treasurer if competent men could be found for the job.

During these years when so much attention was focused upon national and international politics, the Diocese shared the concern of the Church at large in three important matters. The time seemed ripe for a revision of the Prayer Book of 1892. General Convention had set the wheels in motion by appointing a Commission to study and suggest changes. As the reports of this Commission became available they were discussed antd criticized by the clergy. But, since revision was still in its early stages, the matter did not assume a position of prime importance.

It was quite otherwise with the Pension Fund. Up to this time, each Diocese faced the problem of the relief of its retired and disabled clergy and their dependents in its own way, and, of course, very inadequately. In 1913 General Convention determined to set up a Pension Fund on an actuarial basis which would more nearly meet the needs of the superannuated clergy. Its first task was to gather a fund of $5,000,000 which was the minimum amount deemed necessary to assure the successful operation of the plan. When this sum was raised, it would be the responsibility of each Vestry to pay into the fund each year a certain percentage of their Rector's salary.

The quota assigned to this Diocese was $50,000. It seemed at the time a staggering burden, but so successful was the process of education and so appealing the need, that the amount was oversubscribed by $7,000. Other Dioceses were equally successful and in

1917 the money was in hand to set the scheme in motion. With the fund assured, the Diocese worked out the mechanics for co-operating with the plan. The chief question for discussion was whether Vestries should delete the seven and a half percent assessment from their Rector's salary or pay that in addition. The Board of Missions set the example by determining not to penalize the clergy and the parishes followed suit. By 1920, the system was working smoothly and was accepted with a considerable degree of enthusiasm by both clergy and laity.

The war had taught the Church, through the five Liberty Loan Drives and the several drives to raise money for the Red Cross, what could be done by concerted effort, skillful propaganda and effective organization. So, in 1919, General Convention initiated what came to be known as "The Nation-wide Campaign" designed to bring the spiritual and material resources of the Church to bear most effectively and adequately upon her whole task as witness to the Master. It was a program to raise money, and many saw in it little more, but those who conceived the plan thought of it in spiritual as well as material terms. It was in fact in these terms that the greatest results were achieved. In summing up the results, the General Convention of 1922 reported that when the movement began, it revealed the lack of corporate consciousness within the church itself. "We were a congeries of parishes and a too loosely united collection of Dioceses and missionary districts. The campaign brought us together in a remarkable way." They went on to state that "its outstanding feature was the awakening of the whole Church to its opportunity and obligation." Among the tangible results of the campaign we may note that 187 missionaries were sent out, the number of Church School pupils had increased by 24,000, and the teachers by 17,000.

To implement the campaign in the Diocese, a Campaign Committee was appointed under the chairmanship of the Reverend Malcolm DeP. Maynard, Rector of St. John's Church, Bellefonte. Mr. Maynard got a three months leave of absence from his church and opened campaign headquarters in Williamsport in a room furnished by Trinity Parish. Questionnaires were sent to every parish and mission asking them to list their needs and to suggest missionary opportunities. From this survey, a list of the most pressing Diocesan needs was compiled and these were to be the beneficiaries of the funds received during the year. There followed an intensive campaign of education culminating in an Every Member Canvass on December 7. A quota of approximately $76,000 was assigned by the national Church and an additional $79,000 was to be raised for Diocesan purposes. Thus, the sum of about $157,000 was to be raised each year of the Triennium.

In spite of the enthusiasm and hard work of the committee, they could not overcome certain difficulties. One Church officially withdrew from the campaign and several of the smaller places contributed nothing. Some parishes were dissatisfied with the objects designated to receive the benefit of the money; others felt their quotas too large to reach. When Convention met in 1920, the Committee reported that about $66,000 had been pledged—just about forty per cent of the goal. Nevertheless 23 churches met their quota in full, others made a valiant effort and it was felt that had there been more time for preparation, a more successful campaign could have been conducted. Convention discharged the Committee and committed the further conduct of the campaign to the Department of Missions.

Turning now to matters of more local interest, we may note that in 1919, the Diocese assumed control of the Yeates School for Boys. Under the influence of Bishop Bowman, Miss Catherine Yeates had been induced to found and endow the school in 1857 in memory of her father, the Honorable James Yeates, Warden of St. James, Lancaster, and a Justice of the Supreme Court of Pennsylvania. The school was first known as the Yeates Institute of Lancaster and the board of trustees was elected by St. James Vestry whose Rector was President ex-Officio. After getting off to several false starts, the school took root after 1878 and by the beginning of the 20th century was widely known as one of the best board-schools for boys in the Episcopal Church.

While Dr. William F. Shero was Headmaster, the school was moved out of Lancaster to a property along the Fruitville Pike where the students could have the advantages of an athletic field. When Dr. Frederic H. Gardiner became Headmaster in 1899, the school was again moved. The trustees purchased the Eshelman Mill at Greenland along the Lincoln Highway a few miles east of Lancaster. The plot contained 107 acres on which stood a substantial house of Georgian architecture, an old mill, a large barn and several small buildings. The land was studded with beautiful trees and was drained by a stream. Located in one of the most fertile regions of the United States, it was an idyllic setting for a school.

The old mill was converted into a dormitory and the barn into a gymnasium and art room; the smaller buildings were used as living quarters for the faculty and the main house furnished accommodations for the classes. Dr. Gardiner was a splendid educator and able administrator. Under his leadership, boys were attracted from the metropolitan centers and he was successful in increasing the endowment to insure the permanence of the school. During his time, the school reached its peak enrollment of 100 students. Its high academic standards were recognized everywhere and the new era of prosperity was marked in 1903 by a change of name.

As The Yeates School for Boys it attracted students from all over the east. As noted above, the school extended its hospitality to the Board of Religious Education to hold Diocesan Institutes for the Sunday School teachers. Bishop Darlington always visited the school at Commencement time and presented the Bible and Prayer Book prizes and frequently made the Commencement address. Not only did the boys receive a sound preparation for College, but great emphasis was laid upon character education.

But the school also had its troubles. A disastrous fire destroyed the Headmaster's house with all the records of the school. Shortly after the house was rebuilt, the region was visited by a severe cloudburst, the stream overflowed its banks and virtually ruined the property. Dr. Gardiner became discouraged and resigned.

Yet the school continued to operate and, in 1919, seemed on the way to another period of prosperity. By agreement with the Board the Trustees, the Diocese of Harrisburg became responsible for the management of the school and the name was changed to the Yeates Episcopal School of Pennsylvania. It was hoped that under these new auspieces, the school would enter a greater period of usefulness.

During the year 1916, 24 Preaching Missions were held throughout the Diocese, the most outstanding being that held at St. Stephen's, Harrisburg, by Father Huntington, founder of the Order of the Holy Cross. As a possible result of the reawakened spiritual life, three

SAINT JAMES' CHURCH
Lancaster

JAMES HENRY DARLINGTON
Bishop of Harrisburg
1904-1930

new missions were opened in the Diocese during the period: St. Joseph's at Mount Pleasant in Tioga County; St. Patrick's at Mount Union in Huntingdon County; and St. Albert's at Duncannon in Perry County. The latter was a product of the missionary zeal of the Rev. Mr. Dorwart who arranged for the purchase of a property abandoned by the Church of the Brethren near the Juniata bridge at the west end of Duncannon. The church was named in honor of his son Albert, a young man of great promise who had recently died while a student at State College.

Other examples of forward progress were: the admission of St. John's, South Williamsport, as an incorporated parish; the admission of St. Mary's, Waynesboro, as an organized mission; the consecration of St. Barnabas Church, Altoona; St. Peter's, Juniata, and the beautiful St. Paul's Church at Philipsburg. St. Luke's, Altoona, completed and opened their fine new parish house and a fine rectory was built at Riverside. Yet, the Church never quite caught the vision of its Board of Missions nor of its missionaries in the field. Year after year, the Board pleaded for greater financial support to opportunities it could not seize because it could not secure the men. The Rev. Mr. Parchment asked in vain for the rental of a room which could be used as a social center for the colored people of Altoona. Archdeacon Torkington's suggestion for an evangelistic tent to be used in rural areas of Potter and Tioga Counties was ignored.

Some changes in the structure and organization of the Diocese are of interest. In 1916, Tioga and Potter Counties were disassociated from the Archdeaconry of Williamsport and placed in charge of Rev. John W. Torkington, Rector of St. Paul's, Waynesboro, and the district was known as the Northern Archdeaconry. The fiscal year was made to correspond to the calendar year and plans were made for holding the Diocesan Convention in January rather than May. In line with the policy of the general Church which had set up the National Council in 1919, the Diocese in 1920 adopted a canon for the creation of an Executive Council. Beside the Bishop, the council was to be composed of 6 presbyters who were Rectors of parishes, 6 laymen, the Archdeacons and 1 layman elected by each Archdeaconry. The members were to serve for a term of three years and were not eligible for re-election till two years had elapsed. To bring it in line with the organization of the National Council, the following departments were set up: Publicity, Christian Social Service, Religious Education. Work among Colored People, Work among People of Foreign Languages, and the Old Board of Missions was made a Department of the Council. Members of these Departments who were not members of Council were given a seat but not a vote and the Council was to hold at least four meetings during the year.

The years 1915-1920 naturally saw some changes in the leadership of the Diocese. The Diocese suffered a loss in 1916 in the death of Mr. Ivanhoe S. Huber of Shamokin and in 1918 by the death of Rev. Arthur Taylor, Rector of St. John's, York. Two veteran priests, the Rev. Messrs. LeRoy F. Baker and Alexander McMillan, retired. The Venerable Lewis S. Nichols found it necessary because of his health to relinquish his duties as Archdeacon of Williamsport and his place was taken by Rev. Frederick O. Musser; when Mr. Musser left for Chaplain's School, he was succeeded as Archdeacon by Rev. Archibald M. Judd, Rector of All Saints, Williamsport. Mr. McMillan was succeeded at Carlisle by the Rev. Harry D. Viets and as Archdeacon of Harrisburg by Rev. William Dorwart. Mr. Taylor was succeeded at York by the Rev. Paul S. Atkins. The two large Williamsport churches got new Rectors during the period; Rev. Charles N. Tyndall became Rector of Christ Church and Rev. D. Wilmot Gateson, Rector at Trinity. The Rev. George LaScelle succeeded the Rev. Mr. Pugh at Sunbury.

Convention continued to make its round of the churches. Trinity, Williamsport; St. Matthews, Sunbury; St. Paul's, Lock Haven; Trinity, Shamokin, and St. Paul's Philipsburg marked the fifteenth anniversary of the setting apart of the Diocese and the Consecration of Bishop Darlington. In celebration of this event, the Diocese arranged to liquidate the indebtedness of $15,000 on the See House and in appreciation of the work of the Bishop they presented him with a medal inscribed to "The Business Bishop." On the back of the medal, the Diocese gave testimony

1. To the spiritual power of his preaching.
2. To his sympathy and kindness to clergy and laity, both young and old.
3. To his one hundred percent Americanism as acknowledged by the U. S. Congress, and by decorations awarded by foreign countries.

(60)

4. To his business ability shown in the examination of parochial finances and the trebling of missionary monies.
5. To the large increase in the number of communicants and in the value of Diocesan property.

III

"The decade through which America passed from 1919 to 1929" observed Bishop Brown in his address to the Convention of 1932, "had tragic results in the life of our people." Never had prosperity been poured out with such lavish hand upon any nation before. There seemed to be money enough for every citizen. There seemed to be money not only for the necessities, and not only for the luxuries, but even for the whims of young and old alike.

"The war had used up idealism. Our refusal even to consider the League of Nations and the World Court as contributions to the peace of the world showed how ethically bankrupt we had become. The moral fibre of nine out of ten of us in the United States was weakened by war hysteria and warped by the subsequent outpouring of riches.

"Prohibition bore blame for the uprising of the gangster. Scientific discoveries were credited with the infidelity of the week-end pleasure seekers and the neglect of the worship of God. The fundamental cause both of gangsterism in its disregard for the laws of man, and of week-end pleasure seeking in its disregard for the laws of God, was the same, lack of moral earnestness. Flabbiness has come upon our American soul. Dishonesty appeared in high places. The sanctity of the Christian home was threatened throughout the land by the increase of divorce. Children no longer acknowledged the authority of convention and no longer held their fathers and mothers up as ideals to be honored and followed. Looking back on the decade, with its stock market gambling, its lurid emphasis upon sex in film and fiction, its restless discontent, we may well thank God that the crash came when it did.

"The Church suffered in the decade. Not financially, because people gave liberally enough of their overflow to the

Church. But Immortality was lost sight of in the sheer excitement of living here and now. Dependence upon God seemed unnecessary when we had political and industrial leaders promising an ever-ascending scale of money values. History repeated itself in our time and century. 'When the vision fades, the people perish.' The Cross of Christ began to seem foolishness to us who were perishing. Why be unselfish? Isolation is safer. Why be prayerful? Shrewdness and energy will accomplish more. Why be good, when to be happy is a state more easily attained? The American people were on a gayly decorated toboggan, sliding down a spiritual hill, amidst great cheering, having lots of fun. Then came October, 1929. God called His people home."

It was in this atmosphere of confident materialism that Bishop Darligton spent the last third of his Episcopate. He was out of sympathy with the temper of the times and he spoke out against the forces which, not perceived as clearly as in the days of his successor, were surely bringing the country to disaster. In his public utterances, he championed the League of Nations and deplored the fact that his country preferred isolation to co-operation for peace in a world fellowship. He rejoiced, when, at long last, America joined the World Court. He was deeply distressed by the ruthless persecution of the Armenians by the Turks and he gave much time and energy in securing funds to relieve their suffering. He labored diligently to bring about closer relations with the Old Catholics and Eastern Orthodox Churches. In 1925, he was a delegate to the convention of the World Alliance for the Promotion of International Friendship through the Churches. It was his pleasure when travelling abroad to present to distinguished persons Bibles, in the name of the American Bible Society, as a gesture of Christian brotherhood. He constantly urged the people of the Diocese to have respect for the law by cheerful and complete obedience of the Volstead Act. and not to forget God in their new prosperity.

Yet, one cannot deny that on the material side, it was a wonderful decade. Among other things, the automobile became an indispensable part of our American life. Before World War I, it was essentially a plaything. It was used chiefly for pleasure jaunts during

(62)

the summer; roads were so poor that only the boldest would attempt a long journey by car. The War brought the car to full development and at its end, cars began rolling off the assembly line in large numbers. They were much improved and some could be had at so low a price that all but the poorest could own one. As the number of car owners increased, the demand for better roads became more insistent. As a result most of the trunk roads were paved with concrete and longer journeys became practical. In Pennsylvania, Governor Pinchot launched a program to "take the farmer out of the mud" and his program was well along toward completion by the end of the decade.

Naturally, the automobile had profound effects upon our society. The demand for cars virtually absorbed the surplus labor market and attracted many to Detroit, which was to become the automobile capital of the world; thus, many young men who had gone from the Diocese to war found employment in another part of the country.

The railroads soon realized that the automobile was seriously affecting their business as more people began to travel by car and as trucks began appearing on the highway. They began to reduce overhead by consolidating divisions and consolidating the executive staff. This movement was particularly noticed in the Diocese of Harrisburg. Many of the towns depended largely on the railroad for their economic existence, and this consolidation threatened their future. The first shock of this trend was felt by the Episcopal Church. Many of the railroad officials were Episcopalians who gave generous support to the church. When they were removed, the church felt their loss keenly. Altoona, Tyrone, Sunbury, and Renovo were especially hit.

The same tendency for consolidation was seen in the steel industry. As a result the officials of Bethlehem Steel were transferred from Steelton to Bethlehem and the church which at the beginning of the decade was a self-supporting parish paying a salary well above the average, was in charge of a lay reader when the decade ended and its future was quite uncertain.

The automobile affected the church adversely in yet another way. With the shortage of working hours, people had more week-end leisure and they used it to go on trips. This broke the habit of regu-

(63)

lar Church attendance. The Sunday afternoon joyride seriously affected the evening congregation. Thus churches which had to depend on evening services were seriously handicapped. On the other hand, the automobile enabled the clergyman to visit a wider area and serve the church more effectively. Indeed, by the end of the decade the car was as much a part of the clergyman's equipment as his Bible and Prayer Book.

This decade also saw the development of the radio from the primitive crystal set with earphones to a cabinet model operated on ordinary house current; from broadcasts emanating only from Station KDKA to a national hookup. Through this new medium of communication, America adopted new standards of culture, for while the quality of broadcasting was far inferior to present standards, the program material was on a high level. The radio brought the Chautauqua, the concert hall and the lecture course into nearly every American home.

As people became more discriminating in their taste, the church's services came under criticism. After hearing S. Parks Cadman, Harry Emerson Fosdick, or E. J. van Etten, the pulpit efforts of the village preacher suffered by comparison; the trained choirs on the radio accentuated the imperfections of the local volunteer choir. People now felt that they could go to church by radio; the Sunday evening program made a strong bid for the evening congregation. Yet, in towns where there were broadcasting stations, the church had an opportunity to widen its ministry.

A study of the receipts and expenditures of the Diocese during this fabulous period of prosperity showed that Bishop Brown was right in stating that the people gave out of their overflow rather than their abundance. The total Diocesan receipts in 1929 were only some $7,000 greater than they were in 1921. The minimum clergy salary was raised to $2,100 for a parish and $1,800 for a mission. But a study of the salary scale reveals that the clergy did not share in the general prosperity. Three churches did not raise their salaries during the period: St. Luke's, Altoona, paid its clergyman $2,400 and Trinity, Williamsport and St. John's, York, paid theirs $3,600. How the churches reacted to good times is revealed in the following table in which the salaries of the larger churches are noted and a comparison made between the salaries of 1921 and 1929:

(64)

A TABLE OF CLERICAL SALARIES

Place	1921	1929
Altoona (St. Luke's)	$2,400	$2,400
Bellefonte	1,500	2,500
Bloomsburg	1,800	3,000
Carlisle	1,800	2,000
Columbia	1,520	1,720
Harrisburg (St. Andrew's)	1,500	3,000
Harrisburg (St. Paul's)	1,800	2,500
Harrisburg (St. Stephen's)	3,000	4,000
Lancaster (St. James)	4,000	5,000
Lancaster (St. John's)	2,100	3,500
Lewistown	1,500	2,700
Lock Haven	2,200	2,500
Philipsburg	1,800	2,100
Shamokin	1,500	2,400
Sunbury	2,100	2,500
Tyrone	1,360	2,400
Wellsboro	1,400	2,400
Williamsport (Christ Church)	3,750	4,000
Williamsport (Trinity)	3,600	3,600
York (St. John's)	3,600	3,600

Though the Diocese felt it could not meet in full the quota assigned it by the National Council, it felt that it could support an Executive Secretary. This position was created in 1922 and filled by the Rev. Archibald M. Judd. Mr. Judd took care of various promotion programs, supervised the missions, and assisted the Bishop materially in his administrative work. When Mr. Judd resigned in 1928 to become Rector of St. Paul's, Harrisburg, the position was abolished. There was a suggestion that the work be done by a layman, but the suggestion was never acted upon.

In one respect, the Diocese profited by the general prosperity. The small endowment fund had been a source of concern since the establishment of the Diocese. It was felt that the time was now ripe to make a real effort to increase it. In 1923 plans were made to establish a revolving fund of $25,000. When any parish or mission would contribute $50 or any multiple thereof to the endowment, the Diocese would match it from the revolving fund and credit the same to the parish or mission in question. By 1925, the revolving fund had been subscribed and by the end of the period, the endowment fund totalled slightly more than $100,000.

To read the Journals of this period, one would hardly realize that the country was experiencing great social and economic change. The impression is one of "business as usual." The conventions made their rotation of the churches: St. John's, York; St. Stephen's, Harrisburg; St. Luke's, Altoona; St. John's, Lancaster; Christ Church, Williamsport; St. John's, York; St. Matthew's, Sunbury; St. Stephen's, Harrisburg (1927-1928); Trinity, Williamsport, and St. James, Lancaster. In most instances, the proceedings were matters of routine; appointment of committees, election of delegates to General Convention or Provincial Synod, election to membership on various boards and committees, and revision of the canons. But we do note changes in leadership with the passing years.

On the resignation of Mr. Herbert W. Hartman, Mr. Richard M. H. Wharton succeeded as Treasurer of the Diocese and he continued to serve in this capacity throughout the period. On the death of Mr. Munson, in February, 1923, General Clement resigned as Secretary and assumed the position of Chancellor. He was succeeded as Secretary by the Rev. Archibald M. Judd and later by the Rev. Samuel Sayre of St. Mary's, Williamsport.

Two veteran priests passed into larger life. The Venerable Alexander McMillen had been retired, but his counsel was missed in the Diocese after his death. The Venerable William Dorwart died suddenly while serving as Rector at Newport. After his death, interest in St. Albert's at Duncannon which he was instrumental in establishing languished, and by the end of the period the mission was closed. Shortly thereafter, the property was sold for $100.

With the exception of St. James, Lancaster and St. John's, York all the larger churches had a change of Rector. At St. John's, Lancaster, the Rev. George Israel Brown was followed by the Rev. Henry L. Drew, Rev. William T. Sherwood, and the Rev. Frederick P. Houghton.. On the death of the Rev. George W. Gladding Hoyt, who had served fourteen years as Rector at Columbia, Dr. Guy F. Caruthers began a ten-year Rectorship. The long Rectorship of Mr. Sawyer at the Cathedral came to an end with his death in 1925 and

(66)

he was succeeded by Dr. Oscar F. R. Treder of Garden City, Long Island.

George R. Bishop ended a long and fruitful Rectorship at Altoona and his place was taken by the Rev. Richard Allen Hatch. William Heakes was succeeded at Lewistown by the Rev. Thomas Worrall. In Williamsport, D. W. Gateson left Trinity to become Dean of the Pro-Cathedral at Bethlehem and his place was taken by the Rev. Charles E. McCoy. Mr. Tyndall was succeeded at Christ Church by the Rev. Hiram R. Bennett. At Sunbury, George T. LaScelle was followed by Dr. B. Talbot Rodgers and by Rev. Anthony G. Van Elden. At Bloomsburg the Rev. Frederick O. Musser resigned to become Rector at Easton and he was succeeded in turn by Robert R. Morgan and J. Thomas Heistand.

At Philipsburg, the Venerable Franklin T. Eastmant resigned as Rector but continued as Archdeacon of Altoona, and he was succeeded at St. Paul's by the Rev. Charles E. Knickle. Except in the Archdeaconry of Altoona, all the Archdeaconries had a change of leadership. In the Archdeaconry of Harrisburg, Archdeacon Dorwart was succeeded by Paul S. Atkins and then by Alan S. Hughes; in Williamsport, Archdeacon Judd was succeeded by George T. LaScelle, R. R. Morgan, Charles R. Barnes, P. H. Asheton-Martin, and Charles E. McCoy; in the Northern Archdeaconry, Archdeacon Torkington was succeeded by Henry A. Post and Harold E. Schmaus.

One might expect to find this period characterized by church extension in the Diocese, yet this was not the case. St. Bartholomew's, Millersburg, had become so well established by 1922 that it applied for union with the Convention as an organized mission. In 1919, the Rev. Willoughby M. Parchment, who was then ministering to the colored congregation at St. Augustine's, felt that the church would have greater opportunity if it were moved to a new location. With this the Bishop agreed and a new property was acquired at Forster and Cowden Streets. In these larger quarters the congregation functioned as The Church of the Holy Cross. Father Parchment's vision was justified, for by 1925, the church asked to be admitted as an organized mission.

Enola seemed to offer a promising field of endeavor, so, in 1926 the old High School was purchased there and converted into a place of worship. Under the name of St. James, this mission was combined into a circuit with Mechanicsburg, New Market and St. Gerald's, Harrisburg.

The most significant development occurred at State College. The college was growing amazingly, and it was felt that the church could not do the work committed to it without a more adequate plant. Under the leadership of Bishop Talbot, plans were made to raise a fund of $160,000 to build a fine stone church and a parish house. Since students came to the college from all over the state, it was only fitting that all five Dioceses should share in this project. The quota for the Diocese of Harrisburg was $25,000, which was raised without great difficulty. The church was completed in the fall of 1928 and consecrated with appropriate ceremonies on November 9. In recognition of Bishop Talbot's leadership in this undertaking, the tower has been named "The Talbot Tower."

The Department of Christian Education continued to plead for more effective work in the Church School. Each summer it sponsored a training school at Forest Inn at Eaglesmere during the first week in July. Whether the time was inconvenient, the expense too great, the interest lukewarm—perhaps all three—it was observed that registrations grew smaller each year. It therefore seemed the part of wisdom to abandon the project in 1926. Under the auspices of the Girls' Friendly, Betty Washington Camp was established near York. It was the purpose of this camp to provide an inexpensive vacation for the working girls in the towns and cities.

The Yeates School, which had been taken over with enthusiasm in 1919, proved a disappointment. The Diocese assumed responsibility for the school just at the time the state embarked on a program of expansion and improvement of the public High School. Parents were unwilling to spend the money to send their sons to private school when they could receive as good a training at home. All the private preparatory schools knew that they were in a struggle for existence and only the strongest survived. Yeates was a small school; the enrollment never exceeded 100. As registrations declined year by year, Head Masters became discouraged and resigned; with such poor prospects, it was difficult to secure capable administrators. Finally, at a meeting of the Trustees in February, 1929, it was decided to dispose of the property. In 1930, it was sold and it was understood that the money derived from the sale would be used to launch another school at a more favorable location when the time seemed more propitious.

During the decade, the local parish was becoming increasingly conscious of the program of the church at large. During the first few years, it was the Nationwide Campaign that claimed attention. Parishes were being pressed to meet their quotas, which only a few of them did. While Bishop Darlington was disappointed that the Diocese did not come up to expectation, nevertheless he felt that great progress in giving had been made and the effort was well worth while. Parishes became accustomed to the working of the Pension Fund so that arrearages were negligible. Congregations were being introduced to the Hymnal of 1916 which replaced the Hymnal of 1892. Some were using the Hutchins edition with its more familiar tunes and which made little change in the pointing of the chants, while others bought the Pension Fund edition which was better musically and which made a radical departure in the pointing. In 1929, the new Prayer Book became official and the parishes took to it without serious difficulty.

Bishop Darlington was 65 at the beginning of the decade. At an age when many men thought of retirement, he seemed to be in his prime. He travelled constantly throughout the Diocese, and thus became very familiar with conditions in every parish and mission; he knew conditions in many of the homes of his people and it was said that he could call many of the little children by name. He was always available to clergy and laity alike.

He made three trips abroad—to the Lambeth Conference in 1920, and on the same trip was instrumental in having a Concordat between the Anglican and Old Catholic Churches; in 1923, he was absent from February to April on a trip to the Near East and the Holy Land; in 1925, he attended the Congress of Old Catholic Bishops at Berne, Switzerland; on the trip he visited all the Orthodox Patriarchs at his own expense and had the Concordat which had been signed by Bishop Hertzog of the Old Catholic Church in Europe, signed by the Ecumenical Bishop of Constantinople which was confirmed afterward by the Patriarch of Jerusalem sending a letter to the Archbishop of Canterbury.

While he usually spent the summer at Newport, Rhode Island, his diary indicates that they were busy days spent in the service of the Church. The range of his interests was amazing: a closer relation with the Old Catholic and Eastern Orthodox Churches; Near East Relief; The Home for the Aged at Far Rockaway, Long Island; the St. Nicholas Society; The Old New Yorkers; The Pennsylvania Historical and Folklore Society; the Huguenot Society. In all these activities, he exercised a position of leadership.

He always managed to get to New York at Christmas so that he could make the address at the Christmas celebration at Christ Church, Brooklyn, where he had been Rector for twenty-five years. When he read the necrology of Bishops at Convention time, it was of intimate friends of whom he spoke. He knew all the important people in the country, and he was no stranger abroad. Through him, the Diocese was known far and wide, and he brought to the parishes on his annual visitations an experience and vision hard to duplicate.

Amid these varied activities, the Bishop found time for the writing of verse. Some of his poems were written for special occasions, but most were spontaneous outbursts of his sensitive soul. These verses were collected in three volumes and published under the title "Verses By the Way." A poem entitled "Home Coming at Day's End" reflects his attitude to his parish visitations and may serve as a sample of the character of his poetry:

It was Sunday night when the-Bishop returned,
    Coming home on the late evening train;
Three times he'd confirmed, and with whole soul had yearned
    To instruct both in heart and in brain.

Not with wisdom of man, but with God-given love,
    He in three village churches had preached;
Where he earnestly strove to point them above,
    As though Christ, through him, had beseeched.

Each year he had come for the same holy rite
    And laid hands on a score of their youth;
How cheering the sight, boys in black, girls in white,
    Lowly kneeling to pledge faith and truth.

Would many hold out? Would they last to the end?
    His heart answered, "Yes, through God's grace.

God his angels will send, his own to defend
From all that is carnal and base."

That God cares for his flock his own life made him sure,
The peace of believing he knew.
It pays to be pure, and it pays to endure;
Trust God, and you'll find his word true.

He felt strangely tired, and quiet just now;
God had blessed him beyond all his dreams.
"Holy Spirit, do thou with thy fullness endow;
Enlighten my soul with thy beams."

Then asleep in his seat while the train speeded on;
His soul sped still faster to heaven;
To the Land of the Dawn,—for his spirit had gone
Where the souls of God's servants are shriven.

In an article which appeared in "The North American Review" for February, 1928, he set forth "The Joys of the Christian Ministry" in sturdy prose. Recalling his own happy ministry, he pointed out that the life of a minister has many material advantages as well as spiritual joys. Among these material advantages he noted the fact that since a minister is forced to do much reading, his life will always be mentally stimulating; since he must spend much of his time outdoors, his health will improve; he is looked up to in his community and his opinion is sought and respected; he is not bound to a rigid schedule, but can rise and retire at any hour and can take short vacations at will; he has permanent tenure of office; his wife and children are admitted to the best society; his income which is quite adequate is often increased by gifts, by reduced railroad fares and discounts on purchases and by the protection of a pension fund. When this article appeared, no one doubted that it reflected the personal experience of the Bishop but many doubted it as a true picture of the material advantages enjoyed by the average priest. Moreover, many wondered why a Bishop of the Church should place such great emphasis upon the material advantages of this high and holy calling.

But advanced years and constant activity were bound to take their full toll. Realizing this, he asked the Convention of 1928 to give him relief by electing a Suffragan Bishop. A special convention for this purpose met in St. Stephen's, Harrisburg, on February 5, 1929. Most of the aspirants were from the Diocese. The following Diocesan clergy were nominated: The Rev. Messrs. Hiram R. Bennett, Christ Church, Williamsport; Charles E. McCoy, Trinity, Williamsport; Archibald M. Judd, St. Paul's, Harrisburg; Paul S. Atkins, St. John's, York; Lewis Nichols, St. Paul's, Lock Haven; and Charles E. Knickle, St. Paul's, Philipsburg. Another local name—Rev. Oscar F. R. Treder, St. Stephens, Harrisburg—appeared during the balloting. From outside the Diocese the following were placed in nomination: Rev. Messrs. Malcolm D. Maynard, Grace Church, Ridgeway, and a native son: Nathaniel B. Groton, St. Thomas, Whitemarsh; Howard W. Diller, Trinity, Pottsville, and D. Wilmot Gateson, Nativity, Bethlehem, who had served as Rector of Trinity, Williamsport, for five years.

The Convention took twelve ballots without securing an election. Mr. Judd was elected by the clergy from the seventh through the eleventh ballot but he failed to secure the necessary votes of the laity. Since the Convention seemed hopelessly deadlocked, it was decided to adjourn and try again at the regular Convention in the spring.

When Convention met in May, no local men were placed in nomination before the balloting began, but in the course of voting, the names of Messrs. Bennett and Maynard appeared. The nominees this time were: Rev. Messrs. H. N. Arrowsmith, Edwin R. Carter, Lewis G. Morris and Rt. Rev. W. H. Overs. The votes were so widely scattered through five ballots that it was apparent no election was possible and Convention adjourned without giving Bishop Darlington any relief.

As the decade neared its end, the Diocese looked forward to the celebration of its silver anniversary in 1930. A committee of two clergymen and two laymen from each Archdeaconry, under the chairmanship of Dr. Clifford G. Twombly, was appointed to arrange an appropriate celebration. The effect of the stock market crash of 1929 had not been fully felt in the Diocese by the spring of 1930. There seemed every reason to believe that the recession was but a temporary halt to the rising spiral of prosperity. The Convention, therefore, met in a festive mood. There were some anxious moments, however, occasioned by the fact that the Bishop was ill in the hospital early in May and it was feared that his illness might be quite serious, but he was able to leave his bed to preside at Convention and share in the festivities.

In his address, he pointed out that the quarter century had been a period of growth and he bolstered his statement by impressive figures. For example, in 1905, the number of parishes and missions totalled 73; in 1929, 96; in 1905, there were 16,175 baptized persons in 1929, the number was 18,697; the communicant strength in 1905 was 8,303, in 1929, 13,236; 425 persons were Confirmed in 1905 and in 1929, 506; contributions for all purposes totalled $124,964.52 in 1905. In 1929, the amount was $376,904.52—in other words, the people were giving three dollars in 1929 for ever dollar they gave in 1905; 80 men had been ordained to the priesthood; 33 new churches had been built; 46 parish houses were erected; and 34 rectories were either built or purchased. Only in the Church School was there a decline. In 1905, the number of pupils and officers was reported as 5,917; in 1929, it was 5,344.

The celebration took the form of a testimonial dinner held in the ballroom of the hotel Brunswick in Lancaster on the evening of the first day of Convention, May 13. Among the 300 who were present, there were at least eleven who were present twenty-five years earlier when Bishop Darlington was elected. The esteem in which the Bishop was held outside his Diocese is indicated by the letters, telegrams and cablegrams which he received.

Among those sending congratulations were: the Archbishop of Canterbury, the Bishop of London, the Orthodox Archbishop in Brussels, the Patriarch and Pope of the Orthodox Greek Church in Alexandria, Egypt; the head of the Old Catholic Church in the United States and Poland; the Archbishop of the Greek Orthodox Church in America; the Archbishop of the Russian Church in the United States; Frederick C. Morehouse, Editor of "The Living Church," John H. Finley, Editor of "The New York Times"; the Rt. Hon. Sir Gilbert Parket, London; Gen. Smedley Darlington Butler, Washington; Edwin Markham, Staten Island; the Assembly of the Brotherhood of St. Andrew meeting in Elmira; Cynthia W. Alden, President International Sunshine Society; Rabbi Philip D. Bookstaber, Harrisburg; Dr. William F. McDowell, Senior Bishop of the Methodist Church; Bishop Ernest M. Stires, Long Island; Bishop Alexander Mann of Pittsburgh; and Charles M. Schwab.

(73)

The invocation was given by the Rev. Lewis Nichols, President of the Standing Committee, and the Toastmaster was Mr. J. W. B. Bausman, Senior Warden of St. James. First to speak was the Rt. Rev. William Loyal Gravatt, Bishop of West Virginia, who brought the greetings of the House of Bishops. He was followed by the Rev. Dr. Floyd W. Tompkins, Rector of the Church of the Holy Trinity, Philadelphia, who spoke on various phases of the Bishop's life and recalled the friendship of former days in New York. He was followed by Gen. Clement who spoke of the honor and joy it was to serve with the Bishop through the years, and he paid tribute to his sustained effort for the improvement of the Diocese. Bishop Hodur of Scranton recalled the Bishop's efforts in behalf of church unity. Governor Fisher was to have spoken of the Bishop as citizen, but he sent a telegram of regret. Messages were read from President Hoover, Bishop Freeman of Washington and Dr. S. Parks Cadman, former President of the Protestant Council of Churches.

The high point of the dinner was reached when Mr. Richard M. H. Wharton presented in the name of the Diocese, a purse of $2,500.00 which he hoped the Bishop would use for a long contemplated trip around the world or for any purpose he deemed best. He asked the Diocese to express its attitude through those present who stood facing the Bishop and, in the words of the Apostle Peter, they said, "Thou knowest that we love thee." It must have been a moving scene. It is no wonder that the Bishop was overwhelmed.

With the Bishop's Blessing, the meeting adjourned. It was a beautiful ending to twenty-five years of service, and it proved to be a beautiful ending to a relationship that had existed over a quarter of a century. The illness from which the Bishop was suffering at Convention was to be his last. On August 14, word was received that he had died in the hospital at Kingston, New York. The Diocese, the Church, and Christendom knew that a great prophet and leader had gone from them.

It is fitting to close this chapter with an excerpt from an address which Bishop Perry delivered at the Memorial Service for Bishop Darlington held at St. Stephen's Church on November 18:

"A fearless mastery of diverse elements in ways which serve to unify them is the mark of paternal leadership wherever found. The world of science remembers equally with

(74)

HUNTER WYATT-BROWN
Bishop of Harrisburg
1931-1943

JOHN THOMAS HEISTAND
Bishop of Harrisburg
CONSECRATED 1943

filial devotion a Newton, or Pasteur. It is the same quality which gives to the Church a Father in God. The spirit of reconciliation which, in the heart of Bishop Darlington, worked for inter-communion between Christian bodies and which dispelled the differences of a nationality, availed in more intimate pastoral relationships to make of this Diocese a family in Christ. His whole nature responded, as his Episcopate bore witness, to the words of Consecration spoken over him with the laying on of hands: 'God hath not given us the spirit of fear but of power and love.'

"The atmosphere which pervaded his own home and won three sons to the Priesthood has been felt by the great company of communicants who have grown up as his spiritual children in a household of faith. A Diocese which in a quarter century has added one for every year to the number of parishes tells a story of more than administrative force. It speaks of personal devotion and of Apostolic grace.

"The making of disciples, whether they be individuals or congregations, is not soon achieved by conforming to rules of religious propaganda or to the religious habits of a community. It means an uncompromising zeal for Christ, or it means nothing. One who has worked in close association with your Bishop during many years, in many places, has said of him, 'There is no one with whom I have more often disagreed, yet there is no one to whom I would more instinctively turn for understanding sympathy and help in time of trouble.'

"Such testimony to a life of loving leadership and friendship need come from no individual experience. It is rehearsed today in the silence of your own hearts. It rises as in sacrifice of thanksgiving before God for one to whom this Diocese shall ever turn in grateful and loving and sacred remembrance."

Chapter Four

THE SECOND BISHOP OF HARRISBURG

I

The Special Convention which met in Harrisburg November 18 and 19, 1930, to elect a successor to Bishop Darlington assembled with mixed emotions. There was a deep sense of loss, for the Diocese had known no other leadership and that fact was borne in upon the delegates by the address made at the Memorial Service by Bishop Perry. There was also a sense of expectancy, for few of the delegates had had the experience of taking part in the election of a Bishop, and many had come to Harrisburg with rather definite preferences for the man upon whom Bishop Darlington's mantle should fall. Since there was no common preference, sharp cleavages could conceivably develop which would augur no good for the future. For all, there was a sense of strangeness, for the man who had guided the proceedings of the convention through twenty-five years was not in the Chair.

In this situation, it was quite natural for the Convention to choose a familiar figure for its presiding officer. The Reverend Lewis Nichols had been in the Diocese when it was set apart in 1904; he had been a close friend and associate of the late Bishop; he was now President of the Standing Committee. With the wisdom which comes from long experience and with the guidance of the Holy Spirit, he could lead the Convention in the difficult task now lying before it. Patience and good humor would be required a-plenty, for the sharp differences which had blocked two attempts to elect a Suffragan had not been resolved.

At the opening of the Convention, Mrs. Darlington presented the Diocese with a gavel which the Bishop had had carved out of some wood which had been a part of the U. S. S. *Constitution* (Old Ironsides") and Lord Nelson's flagship *Victoria*. The Rev. Samuel Sayre declined to run for the office of Secretary and Mr. Lesley McCreath of Harrisburg was elected to fill the position.

Seven men were placed in nomination for Bishop: Rev. Rudolph E. Brestell of Camden, New Jersey; Rev. Chauncey E. Snowden of Overbrook, Philadelphia; Rev. George T. LaScelle of Oneida, New York; Rev. Henry Harrison Hadley of Syracuse, New York; Rev.

Archibald M. Judd of Harrisburg, Rev. William C. Hicks of Yonkers, New York; and Rev. Robert Scott Chalmers of Baltimore, Maryland.

Balloting began on the morning of the second day. By noon only three ballots has been cast and there seemed no immediate prospect of an election. After an unsuccessful fourth ballot, the names of Messrs. Snowden and Chalmers were withdrawn and the Rev. Squire B. Schofield placed in nomination the Rt. Rev. W. Blair Roberts, Suffragan Bishop of the Missionary District of South Dakota. In order to try to find a way of breaking the deadlock, Convention went into executive session after the sixth ballot. After a recess of an hour, the balloting was resumed with no better results.

After the eighth ballot, Mr. Judd moved to adjourn and that a committee be appointed to receive nominations, study qualifications, and report to the delegates prior to the regular Convention in January. The motion was lost. After two more unsuccessful ballots were taken, a motion to adjourn sine die was defeated. Success came at last on the eleventh ballot, for the President announced the election of the Rt. Rev. W. Blair Roberts. A motion to make the election unanimous was carried, the Doxology was sung, and Convention adjourned.

From the beginning of the balloting, the preference of the laity was for the Rev. Henry Harrison Hadley and he was elected on the lay side from the fourth through the tenth ballots. The clergy at first gave their support to the Rev. Chauncey E. Snowden and, after his name was withdrawn, it was given to Bishop Roberts who was elected by the clergy from the sixth ballot on. Thus, in the final result, the laity bowed to the will of the Clergy.

The following committee was appointed by the President to notify Bishop Roberts of his election: The Rev. Messrs. Hiram T. Bennett, Clifford G. Twombley, Thomas A. Worrall, and Squire B. Schofield, and the Messrs. George S. Schmidt, George A. Gorgas and A. W. Duy.

By arrangements with the Bishop-elect, a meeting was held in Chicago where the opportunities of the Diocese of Harrisburg were presented to him. Bishop Roberts promised to give the matter careful consideration and to give the committee an early answer. In two weeks, Mr. Bennett received a telegram in which Bishop Roberts thanked the Convention for the honor bestowed upon him but stated that he felt called to remain with the Missionary District of South Dakota. The Standing Committee was so informed, and notice was duly given that the chief item of business of the regular Convention of 1931 would be the election of a successor to Bishop Darlington. Thus, the history of the Primary Convention repeated itself.

When the Convention met in York on January 17, 1931, Bishop Darlington still cast a shadow over the assemblage. It was determined to set up a fund which would perpetuate his memory by assisting a project nearest to his heart—the missions of the Diocese. By combining the balance of $29,700 in the Field Work Fund, the $11,541.60 in the Bishop Darlington Fund and a Garage Fund of $1,000, there was a total of $42,241.60 which was ordered to be invested at five percent. The interest on this money was to be used in making grants to missions for capital improvements. Through the years, this fund has enabled missions to make needed repairs and a generation which knew only the name of its first Bishop rose up to call him blessed.

But Convention could not continue to hark back to the past, it must find a new leader. Two local men, Rev. Frederick P. Houghton of Lancaster and Rev. Lewis Nichols of Lock Haven were placed in nomination. Mr. Nichols' nomination was in recognition of his long service to the Diocese and of his able presidency over the Convention, for he never was a serious contender for the office. Two of those who had appeared on the ballot of the previous fall were renominated: Rev. Henry Harrison Hadley of Syracuse and Rev. William C. Hicks of Yonkers. Others named were: Rev. Oliver J. Hart of Chattanooga, Rev. Howard R. Brinker of Chicago; Rev. Lewis G. Morris of Germantown, Philadelphia;; the Very Reverend Wyatt Brown of Buffalo; Rev. H. E. A. Durell of Atlantic City and Rev. W. Appleton Lawrence of Providence, Rhode Island.

The votes were so scattered that no trend was discernible till the fourth ballot when Wyatt Brown was elected by the laity; the clergy, meanwhile divided their support between Frederick P. Houghton and Henry Harrison Hadley. Since the laity were determined to stay by their candidate, the clergy capitulated on the eighth ballot by electing Wyatt Brown by a narrow margin. The election was, of course, made unanimous, and, with thankful hearts, Convention sang the Doxology and adjourned.

The Committee on Notification consisted of Rev. Squire B. Schofield (who nominated Dean Brown), Rev. Frederick P. Houghton, Rev. Oscar F. R. Treder, Gen. Charles M. Clement, Mr. Charles N. Tull and Mr. John J. Evans. Under date of February 3, the Committee received the following letter from the Bishop-elect, written from St. Paul's Cathedral, Buffalo.

"My election to be Bishop of Harrisburg comes unsought and unexpected by me. By a gesture of generous courtesy it was made unanimous.

"My conviction is that God the Holy Ghost ruled over the Convention, and that the result is in accordance with the divine will. I realize my many limitations, but am confident that the Lord Jesus Christ who calls me to this task in His Church will grant me strength and wisdom sufficient to make up what I lack, and enable me faithfully to perform the duties of this high office. On Christ I rely day by day.

"Therefore, subject to all canonical requirements, being met, and expressing due appreciation for the confidence placed in me, I hereby accept my election.

Wyatt Brown.

While the Standing Committee awaited the canonical consent of the Bishops and Standing Committees to his election before arranging for the consecration of the new Bishop, the people of the Diocese were gathering such information as they could about him. They could readily discover that he was born at Eufaula, Alabama, on February 14, 1884 and consequently, he would be a man of forty-seven.

He had received his collegiate and seminary training at the University of the South at Sewannee, Tennessee from which he received the degree of B.A. in 1905 and B.D. three years later. He was ordered Deacon upon graduation and advanced to the priesthood in 1909. In 1911, he married Miss Laura Little of Montgomery. In 1908, he was Assistant at St. John's, Montgomery; in 1909, he was briefly in charge of St. Mark's, Prattsville, Alabama; and from 1909-13, he was Rector at All Saints', Mobile. He was then called to Asheville, North Carolina, where he was Rector of Trinity Church which he served for two years.

(80)

In 1915, he was honored by the University of Alabama with the degree of Doctor of Letters. That same year, he became Rector of the Church of the Ascension, Pittsburgh where he remained for five years. He was called to Baltimore in 1920 to be Rector of the Church of St. Michael and All Angels. He had been in his present position as Dean of St. Paul's Cathedral, Buffalo since 1928. Thus, while a Southerner born and bred, he had lived long enough in the North to feel at home and since he had spent the last fifteen years on the borders of the Diocese of Harrisburg, he was not unacquainted with its problems and opportunities.

The Consecration was set for St. Philip and St. James Day in St. Stephen's Church. The following committee was appointed to make arrangements for the service: The Rev. Oscar F. R. Treder, Chairman; the Rev. Messrs. Lewis Nichols, Paul S. Atkins, Clifford G. Twombley, Charles E. McCoy, and the Messrs. Richard M. H. Wharton, Frank Payne, Lesley McCreath and J. Allen Donaldson.

As it was the first Consecration to be held within the Docese, the event naturally drew many people to Harrisburg on that Friday morning in early May, for the people were not only eager to have a look at their new Bishop but were anxious to take part in and witness the solemn ceremony in which he was set apart.

The impressive procession moved into the church to the singing of "Rise, Crowned With Light"; "O 'Twas a Joyful Sound to Hear"; and "Glorious Things of Thee Are Spoken". The procession moved in three divisions each preceded by a Crucifer and marshalled respectively by the Rev. Messrs. Squire B. Schofield and Hiram R. Bennett, Arthur G. W. Pfafko and J. Thomas Heistand, Frederick P. Houghton and Clifford W. French.

The first division was the Procession of Guests consisting of the Choir, Seminarians, Ministers of Protestant Churches, Clergy of the Eastern Orthodox Church, Clergy of Other Dioceses.

The second division was the Procession of the Diocese, made up as follows: The Clergy in the order of seniority of ordination, Officers of the Diocese, The Treasurer, The Chancellor, The Vestry of St. Stephen's Church, The Standing Committee, the Rector of St. Stephen's.

The last division, the Procession of the Bishops, moved in the following order: Bishops of the Eastern Orthodox Churches, Bishops of the Protestant Episcopal Church, the Bishop of Lexington, the Bishop-elect with his attending Presbyters; the Rev. Bertram E. Brown, Rector of Calvary Church, Tarboro, North Carolina and the Rev. Francis F. Lynch of St. Paul's Cathedral, Buffalo; The Bishop of Maryland; the Bishop Coadjutor of Western New York; the Bishop of Central New York; the Bishop of Delaware; the Presiding Bishop.

When all were in their places, the Rt. Rev. James DeWolf Perry, Presiding Bishop, began the service of Holy Communion by reading the Collect appointed for the Consecration of a Bishop. After the singing of the Nicene Creed, the Rt. Rev. Henry Pryor Almon Abbot, Bishop of Lexington preached the sermon. Then the Rt. Rev. Edward Trail Helfenstein, Bishop of Maryland and the Rt. Rev. Cameron J. Davis, Bishop Coadjutor of Western New York presented Dean Brown to the Presiding Bishop with the words: "Reverend Father in God, we present unto you this godly and well-learned man to be Ordained and Consecrated Bishop."

In support of this presentation, the following testimonials were read: the Certificate of Election, by Rev. Lewis Nichols; the Canonical Testimonial, by Rev. Charles E. McCoy; the Certificate of Ordinations, by Rev. Paul S. Atkins; the Consents of the Standing Committees, by Mr. Lesley McCreath, and the Consents of the Bishops by the Rt. Rev. David L. Ferris, Bishop of Western New York. In response to the Presiding Bishop's request, the Bishop-elect then made the following solemn declaration: "In the name of God, Amen. I, Wyatt Brown, chosen Bishop of the Protestant Episcopal Church in the Diocese of Harrisburg, do promise Conformity and obedience to the Doctrine, Discipline and Worship of the Protestant Episcopal Church in the United States of America. So help me God, through Jesus Christ." Then, the Presiding Bishop having moved the congregation to pray, the appropriate Litany was read by the Rt. Rev. Alexander Mann, Bishop of Pittsburgh.

After the examination of the Candidate and the singing of "Veni Creator Spiritus", the high point of the service arrived. The presiding Bishop, the Rt. Rev. Charles Fiske, Bishop of Central New York, and the Rt. Rev. Philip Cook, Bishop of Delaware laid their

(82)

hands on Dean Brown and consecrated him Bishop in the Church, saying:

Receive the Holy Ghost for the Office and Work of A Bishop in the Church of God, now committed unto thee by the Imposition of our hands; In the Name of the Father, and of the Son, and of the Holy Ghost. Amen. And remember that thou stir up the grace of God, which is given thee by this Imposition of our hands; for God hath not given us the spirit of fear, but of power, and love, and soberness.

Then the Presiding Bishop, delivering him the Bible continued:

Give heed unto reading, exhortation, and doctrine. Think upon the things contained in this Book, Be diligent for them, that the increase coming thereby may be manifest unto all men; for by so doing thou shalt both save thyself and them that hear thee. Be to the flock of Christ a shepherd, not a wolf; feed them, deliver them not. Hold up the weak, heal the sick, bind up the broken, bring again the outcasts, seek the lost. Be so merciful, that you be not too remiss; so minister discipline, that you forget not mercy; that when the Chief Shepherd shall appear, you may receive the never-fading crown of glory; through Jesus Christ our Lord. Amen.

Following the vesting of the Bishop and the investiture with his staff of office, the service of the Holy Communion was continued. After the singing of "Gloria in Excelsis" and just before the Blessing, the Presiding Bishop offered a prayer in these words:

Most merciful Father, send down, we beseech thee, upon this thy servant thy heavenly blessing; and so endue him with thy Holy Spirit, that he, preaching thy Word, may not only be earnest to reprove, beseech, and rebuke, with all patience and doctrine, but also may be, to such as believe, a wholesome example in word, in conversation, in love, in faith, in chastity, and in purity; that, faithfully fulfilling his course, at the latter day he may receive the crown of righteousness laid up by the Lord Jesus, the righteous Judge, who liveth and reigneth with thee and the same Holy Spirit, one God, world without end. Amen.

As the congregation moved out of the church, they knew that they had had an experience which they would not soon forget. "Surely, God was in this place." The words of the Presiding Bishop's final prayer found echo in the heart of everyone there in the words of the offertory anthem:

O Wisdow, Spirit of the Holy God,
Effulgent glory of eternal light,
Thou order'st all things, O divinest Might,
Strong Wisdom, Spirit of the Holy God.

O Sovereign Lord, Thou Master of Man's souls,
Inspire, we pray thee, by thy human Name
Man's feeble will with love's perpetual flame,
And hold the wheels of life with strong control.

O steadfast Spirit of the Holy God,
O come, be near us, guide us day by day,
With saving hand along thy marvelous way,
Fair Wisdom, Spirit of the Holy God.

II

The first impact the new Bishop made upon the Diocese came with the announcement that St. Stephen's Church, Harrisburg, would be the Cathedral Church. The initiative in this did not come from the Bishop but from St. Stephen's. The Vestry of the parish offered their church to the Bishop for his Cathedral, and the Bishop gladly accepted the offer. It was clearly understood that the change of status would not prejudice any of the rights of the parish nor interfere with any of the prerogatives of the Vestry. Henceforth, the Rector of St. Stephen's would be the Dean of the Cathedral; and the Cathedral Chapter would consist of the Bishop, the Dean, the Chancellor of the Diocese, St. Stephen's Vestry, and five honorary Canons. The first such Canons to be appointed were: Rev. Paul S. Atkins of York; Rev. Hiram R. Bennett of Williamsport; Rev. Clifford W. French, the Bishop's Secretary and Chaplain; Rev. Richard Allen Hatch of Altoona; and Rev. Clifford G. Twombley of Lancaster.

The announcement was greeted with enthusiasm by a Diocese which saw in this change a sign of maturity and progress. The

(84)

Cathedral belonged to all the people; it was the focal point at which the Diocese could meet on common ground; it was the visible sign of that unity which is so necessary for the efficient functioning of a Diocese. Without feeling that they were imposing unduly upon the hospitality of a parish, the various committees and departments could have a place of meeting which was their own. Moreover, it was the natural place for holding the annual convention. Thus, the practice of rotating the conventions among the larger churches which had been in vogue since the beginning of the Diocese was discontinued and all conventions during Bishop Brown's administration were held at the Cathedral except that of 1941 when Convention accepted the invitation of Christ Church, Williamsport to sit there as a feature of the celebration of the one hundredth anniversary of the establishment of that parish.

But it was only as the Bishop made his visitations that the Diocese began to know him as a person. Those who had the privilege of entertaining him in their homes found him a delightful and considerate guest who put people at their ease and delighted them with his witty and pleasant conversation. At parish gatherings, his stories (of which he seemed to have an inexhaustible fund) linked him with his people and through the medicine of laughter heavy hearts became lighter. In his early visitations, he delighted to tell of his two sons, one of whom was "six foot two" and the other "two foot six."

But it was in the services of the church that the Diocese first discovered that they had a true father in God. Those who were presented for confirmation will never forget the solemnity with which the Bishop's Chair was brought forward, nor the awesomeness of his tone as he inquired of the candidates: "Do ye here in the presence of God. . ." nor could they but be moved by the sincerity with which he uttered the Confirmation prayer in which he invoked the sevenfold gifts of the spirit upon those upon whom he was about to lay his hands. And they would long remember the little addresses made to them when the service was over based on the motto he had selected for the classes of that year. Such mottos as "My defense is of God" gave challenge and encouragement to those who were entering into a new relation with the Church.

In the pulpit, the Bishop spoke with an eloquence reminiscent of the orators of the Old South, with a depth of conviction characteristic of the Old Testament prophets and yet with winsomeness that marked him a servant of Jesus Christ. When the world seemed to be tumbling at man's feet as it did in the '30's, when men were seeking to make the difficult adjustment to new standards of living and new patterns of thought, it was heartening to hear him speak with such confidence of "the things which cannot be shaken."

As a leader of the Diocese, he kept the vision before it, yet he never demanded the impossible. As a presiding officer, he showed tact, judgment, and patience, all exercised in a spirit of genial good humor. He was swift to praise and slow to condemn. He asked no sacrifice which he himself would not make; he laid no heavier burden upon his Diocese than he was willing to bear. His faith assured him that however dark the clouds, the sun still shone; in the worst of times, he kept his faith in the best; man might fall but God who had been our help in ages past was our hope for years to come.

He had the gracious hospitality represented by the best traditions of the South. "Bishop's Court is yours," he said repeatedly on his parish visitations as he urged the people to call on him when in Harrisburg. It was his custom to invite the delegates to tea at his home on the adjournment of every convention. His hospitality was shared by his good wife who frequently invited the wives of the delegates to luncheon while their husbands were attending to the sober business of the Church.

Unlike Bishop Darlington, he devoted the major part of his time and attention to the affairs of the Diocese. He spent his vacations at Blue Ridge Summit where Dennystead had been presented to him as a summer residence. Aside from the responsibilities placed upon him by the House of Bishops and General Convention, his only extra-Diocesan activity entailed being President of the Third Province—a position to which he was elected in 1941.

The clergy found him both a father in God and a loving brother. He was always zealous for their welfare, urging that the parishes and missions provide adequately for their comfort. At every convention, he called attention to the fact that in this Diocese there was a group of clergy second to none, of whose loyalty he could not speak too highly. On one occasion, he displayed his fatherly concern by counselling them to be careful to speak kindly of one another, to avoid the spirit of faction and jealousy which will destroy the unity which is the Church's strength.

Both the Diocese and the people of central Pennsylvania discovered that the Bishop was an outspoken patriot. Like his predecessor, he deplored the fact that the United States had preferred isolation to joining the League of Nations, and the materialism had given place to idealism. He warned against the danger to the world at large in the aggression of Hitler and Mussolini. He saw more clearly than many that the rise of dictatorships was a threat to freedom everywhere. He was so outspoken in his denunciation of neutrality and his advocacy of preparedness that he was put down in some quarters as a war monger. In an address delivered to the Diocese of Pennsylvania at their Convention in Philadelphia in May, 1941, he was severely criticized for stating that our children's children would pay dearly for our policy of neutrality. Yet nothing could shake him from his conviction and subsequent events proved him right. While he subscribed to the Christian ethic of turning the other cheek in cases of personal injury, he held that Christ would not have His Followers stand by idle while others were being injured. "He that is an hireling and not the shepherd, whose own the sheep are not, seeth the wolf coming and fleeth, and the wolf catcheth them and scattereth the sheep. The hireling fleeth because he is an hireling, the good shepherd giveth his life for the sheep."

His attitude is well illustrated by what he said to his last Convention in 1943:

"A reverent reading of history strengthens the faith of a Christian in the ultimate triumph of Right. Battles may be lost to Cruelty and Wrong, but the War is always won by those on the side of Justice and Liberty and the Welfare of the Human Race. Therefore, in this present conflict where the issues between Right and Wrong are clearly drawn, we are absolutely confident that, though battles have been lost and will be lost, the ultimate triumph of the United Nations is assured.

"We believe this, and the majority of our fighting men in the Army and Navy believe it, not because God is on our side. He does not play favorites among his children. But we and they believe it because God the Father has revealed to us in his Incarnate Son that He is a God of Liberty, not slavery; of Pity not Cruelty, of Justice not Persecution. And the United Nations are battling for these things.

"In other words, we shall conquer in the Sign of the Cross. That Sign is a Sign of good emerging out of evil. The Cross with our Dear Lord's Figure upon it stands for suffering in the cause of Right. But the empty Cross and the empty Tomb stand for the triumuph of Love over Evil that men may do. The United Nations will surely win this war because they are on God's side and on the side of His suffering children everywhere."

The Bishop was also a stout defender of the faith. He was greatly disturbed by the constant tampering with the Marriage Canon by General Convention. He deplored the liberalizing of the Church's legislation and insisted that when the matter was settled by one convention it should not be made a continual subject of discussion. While he ardently wished for the healing of schism which had rent the Church asunder at the Reformation, he felt that it should not be sought at the expense of the tenets of the Catholic Faith which the Church had held from the beginning.

In the late '30's and early '40's, there was a strong movement in the church to seek organic unity with the Presbyterians. With this movement, the Bishop was not in sympathy. His mind is reflected in this excerpt from the address which he made to the Convention of 1943:

" . . . . We all long for a healing of the wounds that have been made in the Mystical Body of Christ. We all agree that Christians should be one in spirit and in truth.

"But organic unity between a Branch of Christ's One, Holy Catholic and Apostolic Church with a Church which has separated itself from both Catholic Faith and Practice involves much more than a sentimental longing for peace. The Church of England and all her daughters in the Anglican Communion have inherited as a sacred trust in the treasure of Apostolic Succession and of a Sacramental System that is not only declarative but also effective through the power of the Holy Ghost.

(88)

"Our Personal conviction is that should the Diaconate, and Apostolic Order of the Sacred Ministry and Confirmation, named by St. Paul as one of the essentials of the Faith and so considered throughout the long history of the Christian Church be sacrificed for union with the Presbyterians, this union would be a betrayal of our trust. Baptismal Regeneration, the Real Presence of Christ in the Holy Eucharist and the order of Priesthood are essential to the Faith also, which cannot be lightly disregarded.

"To our mind, the Methodist Church which is a daughter of the Church of England and is in the Anglican tradition, would have been a far better prospect for organic union. Because the women of two churches belong to the same social set and their laymen sit together at the same directors' tables there is not guarantee of theological affinity. We have rarely met a Presbyterian minister who cared particularly about union with the Episcopal Church. We have, however, during our ministry met countless numbers of Methodist ministers who expressed themselves as feeling the need of Apostolic Succession and longed to regain that Anglo-Catholic faith and practice which Methodism loved long since but lost awhile."

There can be no doubt that the Bishop had won his way into the heart of his Diocese. When ill health forced his retirement in 1943, the announcement forced the Diocese to put its thoughts in words. Canon Atkins expressed the mind of the Diocese in these words of loving tribute:

"Coming to Harrisburg twelve years ago, in the darkest days of the depression, bringing the rich resources of a long and brilliant ministry in some of the largest Parishes of our Church, Bishop Wyatt-Brown immediately endeared himself to us all. His friendly nature and overflowing heart enkindled a flame of affection that united us, as never before, in the bond of Christian love. His appreciation and encouragement stimulated both Clergy and Laity alike to new and greater endeavor for Christ and His Church. His Parish visitations, always a Benediction, were eagerly anticipated. His staunch loyalty communicated itself to his people, quickening in them a deeper sense of pride in our Parishes and Diocese. His ministry among us was with power because he never lost in the Episcopate the pastoral touch. In the light and warmth of his glowing faith and Apostolic zeal the darkness of depression dissolved.

"A gracious Bishop and Shepherd of our souls, a true Father in God to all, an able Administrator, a forceful and eloquent Preacher of Righteousness, a Prophet proclaiming fearlessly the Word of Truth with power, a Watchman warning without equivocation an endangered Nation, when its citizens were dazed and divided by a multitude of conflicting and confusing voices, we feel justly proud of this holy and humble-hearted man of God who dared to speak the truth boldly, when outspoken preaching was condemned and resented by a thoughtless and heedless people.

. . . .

"Nor can we overlook the lovely lady, and charming helpmeet who by his side has borne the burden and heat of the day, whose joy and satisfaction in the full fruition of the Bishop's ministry we share. Mrs. Wyatt-Brown's gracious hospitality, her valued leadership in the Woman's Auxiliary, her helping hand in all good works, have enriched our Diocesan life, and will remain a treasured remembrance among us."

III

It took courage to accept a call to be Bishop of Harrisburg in 1931. The stock market crash was only an interesting news item to most people in central Pennsylvania in 1929. They believed the assurances given them from Washington that such setbacks as business was suffering were only temporary, that the country was passing through a period of necessary adjustment that would soon pass. By 1931, however, even the most confirmed optimist knew that the country was experiencing its worst depression, nor were they much cheered by the news that "prosperity was just around the corner." Many had lost their savings through bank failures; others had their assets frozen in banks which were in the process of liquidation. Men who had been laid off could find no other employment, and their situation was desperate because no well organized program of relief had yet been formulated. Businessmen found inventories piling up; those who were still employed found slips in their pay envelopes notifying them that their salaries had been cut; school teachers who believed that at long last their inadequate salaries would buy them a comfortable living discovered that their school boards were so financially embarrassed that they could not pay them at all. Young people who had gone off to the city to work during the plush days of prosperity now came home to add to the burden of their parents. People might laugh at the statement that "depression means getting along without what our fathers never had," but there was little mirth in the laughter.

Such conditions brought serious problems to the church. There was the spiritual problem of those whose faith had been based on the security of material possessions and who had discovered that they had built their house upon the sand. To admit their folly, was not easy; it was more comforting to blame their misfortune upon God. Others, who had honestly sought to build wisely, and who were now suffering through no fault of their own, felt that God had let them down. The church had to be patient with these people, it had to restore faith in a God who changes not and who still cares for his children though they suffer. The church had to speak courage to the discouraged, hope to the despairing. Above all, it needed to give a sane interpretation of what had happened, and the words of the Bishop gave an example to the church of what she needed to say:

"The Providence of the Heavenly Father is over all his children. There is no peculiar people. There are no favorite sons in the Household of God. The Almighty loves all nations, and those who seem to be loved most, are simply those which are best able to receive and most able to reciprocate that outpouring of divine devotion. Therefore, the suffering of a part, sooner or later, brings agony to the whole brotherhood of man. America's depression, though delayed, was sure to come, because America was part of the depressed and broken world. There can be no security for anybody unless there be security for everybody. The billionaire and the breadline inevitably menace each other. Even though, by better distribution, the wealthy lose something of their gain, in the long run the lesser hours of labor and higher wages of the masses will make for the good of those who seem to lose. . . .

.   .   .   .

"The homely virtues of faith and fidelity, fortitude and courage, honesty, and purity, are still valid. Homes wrecked by selfishness and lust, commercial institutions bankrupt by greed and fraud, the Church of Christ made desolate by skepticism and apathy, have proven poor foundations upon which American liberty expected to rest and endure.

". . . The purpose of worship stands forth in clearer light today against the background of gloom than it did when the radiance of prosperity made it faint and dim. The purpose of Worship is to admire and adore the perfect character of God as revealed in Jesus Christ our Lord. The purpose of Worship is so to admire and adore that men long to surrender themselves in obedience and devotion so they may become like Him before Whom they bow. Men who no longer worship God as revealed in Christ, no longer desire to become like Him, and no longer desiring to become like Him, they no longer attain to His likeness. The world's greatest need, America's greatest need, is more men and women who go about doing good and being good, as our Lord Christ did and was, when incarnate on this earth."

Equally serious, and in some respects more serious because the effect was more immediate, was the financial problem. In the days of prosperity, it was easy to persuade people to give generously of their overabundance, but when it became necessary to practice rigid economy, a people who had not been trained to give sacrificially, naturally felt that economy could well begin in their contributions to the church. As a result, parish budgets had to be cut drastically, repairs long overdue were postponed, and some churches even neglected the pension premiums of their clergy not realizing that through their delinquency the pension of every priest of the Diocese was put in jeopardy. In the case of two churches, the matter became so serious that the interest charge was greater than the principal sum owed. It was not until 1948 that these arrearages were finally cleared up and the Diocese had a clean slate with the Pension Fund.

(92)

When it was so difficult to meet current expenses Vestries often postponed the payment of the church's Diocesan assessments. According to canon, churches who thus failed were disqualified from voting in Convention, and it became common for the Finance Committee, after reporting the arrearage, to recommend that the churches in question be forgiven and that their voting rights be restored. In some cases it was felt that no such leniency could be granted and as a result some churches found themselves deeply in debt to the Diocese. For illustration, the following delinquencies were reported to the Convention of 1938:

St. Lukes, Altoona	$ 351.41
St. James, Bedford	216.88
St. Paul's, Harrisburg	438.48
St. Mark's, Lewistown	1,514.96
Trinity, Shamokin	1,054.52
Trinity, Steelton	227.32
St. Paul's, Wellsboro	347.40
All Saints', Williamsport	454.60

The Diocese faced the facts realistically, and in view of conscientious effort to meet present assessments, wrote off past arrearages and gave the churches a clean slate.

This unhappy condition pointed up the fact, often called to the attention of Convention, that from its inception the Diocese had been operating with an insufficient endowment fund. The Bishop met this situation courageously by asking the Convention of 1932 to cut his $9,000 salary by ten percent and all the paid Diocesan officers followed his example. But there was patent need that the fund be increased. With so great an extent of territory, it was physically impossible for a Bishop to give the Diocese the spiritual care and administrative oversight it deserved.

Several measures of relief were open. A paid Archdeacon could be employed, or a Suffragan or Coadjutor elected and consecrated. An increased endowment would make this possible. Accordingly in 1936 the Bishop appointed a committee of twenty-two under the Chairmanship of the Rev. J. Thomas Heistand to seek to enlarge the fund by $134,000. It was clearly understood that any moneys subscribed could be credited either to the Diocese as a whole or to the individual parishes of the donor as he might direct. In spite of their best efforts, this committee was not able to increase the fund appreciably.

But it was the Field Work Fund that suffered most. Believing that most of this money was for foreign missions and not realizing that the mission priests of the Diocese were largely dependent upon it for their support, contributions fell off sharply. To remedy this situation somewhat, all quotas were cut ten per cent and the Diocesan aid to its missionaries was cut correspondingly. Then, too, the missionary work in the Diocese was evaluated more critically. It became a matter of serious concern to the Diocese as to whether it was right to pour money into places which for a long period had shown little sign of growth. After very careful study and serious consideration, the following churches were closed during Bishop Brown's administration:

St. John's, Catawissa
St. James, Enola
Christ Church, Everett
Good Shepherd, Galeton
St. Nathaniel's, Natalie
St. Chrysostom's, New Market
Grace Church, Nickel Mines
Mount Olivet, Nordmont

St. Gerald's, Harrisburg, was closed as a white mission and the congregation of the Church of the Holy Cross having given up their rooms on Forster Street, moved up on the hill and took over St. Gerald's. One is struck by the fact that this is not only a story of financial stringency but of lost opportunity. Had priest and people had greater commitment, some of these churches might have been saved. More visitation in the home might have saved the situation. This was certainly in the Bishop's thought which he often expressed privately to the clergy and, on the occasion of Dr. Twombly's retirement, spoke of it publicly:

"Before we leave the subject of the state of the Church in the Diocese of Harrisburg, we must run the risk of being monotonous by emphasizing, both to the clergy and the lay-readers of each parish and mission, the importance of visitations to the home. In olden days the path of the penitent in the Church led from his own doorstep to the confessional and the priest. Every priest had an intimate knowledge of the life, the fears, the sins and heartbreaks, the desires for forgiveness and renewal of each and every one of his people.

"We all know that this is no longer a factor in the average parish or mission of the Episcopal Church. Very few go voluntarily to the priest to seek spiritual counsel and the absolution of God. Therefore, 'if the mountain will not come to Mohammed, Mohammed must go to the mountain.' The path still exists between the altar and the doorstep, but the feet of the Man of God must make the journey. We consider it imperative that every clergyman visit his people unremittingly, lovingly and in the name and spirit of His Master.

"He should pray with his people and should invite them to open their hearts to him as the representative of their Lord and of his Holy Church. He should keep a record, accurate as to date, of every visitation, in order that he may avoid the pitfall of calling ofttimes upon the congenial and rarely or never upon the recalcitrant and wayward and wandering sheep.

"It grieves us, as we go about the Diocese, to hear this complaint concerning our clergy. Laymen rightfully feel that the priest does not earn his living when he does not shepherd his flock. Where one priest fails to build up his church and satisfy the spiritual longing of his people because of physical or mental deficiency, ten priests fail because of inertia or lack of method in the proper apportioning of their time day by day in the service of God."

While it is impossible to fix the blame for the lack of growth in the missions, it was clear to every one that something needed to be done about the method of raising the funds to support them. Even in good times, missionary giving had fallen far short of the needs. As we have seen, the situation in depression times, was little short of tragic. In 1938, Mr. John I. Hartman of Lancaster, proposed a plan to Convention which he believed would greatly improve the situation. Heretofore, each parish and mission was assigned a missionary apportionment which was treated like the Diocesan assessment, and failure to meet this apportionment disqualified the parish or mission from voting in the Convention. The Hartman Plan would change missionary giving from a tax to a voluntary gift: While missionary giving was as much an obligation as the Diocesan assessment, it should be paid not out of coercion but out of a loving heart eager to obey the Lord's command to go and teach all nations. He felt that the plan would raise missionary giving from a material to a spiritual plane. If the plan was adopted, each parish would assume whatever quota it chose depending upon its ability and consecration. To make the plan effective, there would, of course, have to be a good program of missionary education.

Churches were given guidance as to the amounts they ought to give by being presented a mathematical quota which, if every parish and mission would meet, the missionary budget would be subscribed. Churches that exceeded this quota were to be classified as A, AA and AAA; those that fell short were classified as B, C, and D. Convention thought highly of the plan and adopted it. The first so-called "normal quotas" were ascertained by taking 18 percent of the parochial expenses for the preceding three years: parishes that gave 18 percent and 25 percent were to be in Class A, those that gave between 25 percent and thirty-three and one-third percent were to be in class AA and those that gave one third or more of their parochial budget to missions were considered in Class AAA. Churches which gave between 15 percent and 18 percent were to be in Class B, those who gave between 10 percent and 15 percent were in Class C, while those who gave less than 10 percent were in Class D. This plan was thoroughly explained at various missionary rallies throughout the Diocese and it met a good response.

By 1935, the nation was well on the way to recovery. As central Pennsylvania felt the effects of the depression late, so it was slow in being caught up in returning prosperity. But, by 1935, everyone knew the worst was over and people began to look forward with confidence to better days. But calamity was not finished with the Diocese of Harrisburg. On St. Patrick's Day, 1936 the waters of the Juniata and Susquehanna and their tributaries swelled to flood proportions, carrying destruction to the towns and cities along their banks. Many of our people lost heavily and some of the churches suffered serious damage. Perhaps the most seriously crippled communities in the

(96)

Diocese were Tyrone, Lock Haven, Williamsport, Sunbury and Harrisburg. At Lock Haven tragedy struck double. The flood was ruining St. Paul's Church, when in some mysterious way, fire broke out and virtually destroyed the church. This second tragedy proved a blessing in disguise, for the parish was insured against fire and the insurance money greatly aided the parish in its rebuilding program. Since flood insurance is unobtainable, other parishes damaged by the flood were obliged to shoulder the expenses of their rehabilitation. In 1938 fire completely destroyed the inside of St. John's, Lancaster.

Strangely enough, the flood did not seem to discourage the people of the Diocese, it acted as a spur to greater effort, it was the crisis which was necessary to arouse the people from the despair into which the depression had plunged them. In an incredibly short time, the damage was repaired and parishes had not only new and more beautiful churches, but in the struggle to rebuild the people found new spiritual vitality.

Still, the sun could not break through the clouds. In the closing years of the decade, peace in Europe became more uneasy as the totalitarian states continued to advance their empires at the expense of the free world. Across the Pacific, there was war in China and Japanese aggression seemed a threat to democratic developments in the Far East. War clouds were surely gathering and the United States did not delude itself into believing that it could escape should the world be once more engulfed in war. Accordingly, preparations were made for defense, and the various services greatly increased their personnel. A new prosperity came to America and it was evident that the spiritual lessons learned in the depression were being rapidly forgotten. While the possibility of war was very real in the country, the nation was not prepared to receive the news on Sunday afternoon, December 7, 1941, that Japan had struck at Pearl Harbor. The days of anxious waiting were over, World War II had come to America.

The effect of America's entrance into the war was soon apparent in the parish life of the Diocese. Three churches found themselves without Rectors when the Rev. Earl M. Honaman of St. Paul's, Bloomsburg, the Rev. W. Josselyn Reed of St. Paul's, Columbia, and the Rev. Donald C. Means of St. Paul's, Harrisburg entered the service as Chaplains. Young men and women from every parish

(97)

were leaving home to don the uniform of their country. Romances accelerated in tempo with the prospect of early induction. In every parish church, service flags were displayed with an ever lengthening line of blue stars, some of which erelong were to be replaced with gold. In industrial communities, Sunday was no longer a day of rest and church attendance suffered. Civilian war work pre-empted much of the time of the women to the detriment of church organizations. Travel restrictions discouraged Diocesan meetings, and food rationing virtually put an end to the serving of church suppers. Inflation was boosting prices and wages but the lag between the two with the increasing tax burden made the cost of living a serious problem.

The task of the church was to keep the issues clear, to keep faith alive and to bind up hearts broken by anxiety and tragedy. To this task the Bishop addressed himself, and to this task he inspired his people.

Yet the picture was not all dark. In the year 1932, when the depression was at its worst, 157 more confirmations were reported than in any year during the previous decade. The large number of young people who found difficulty filling in their time awakened the Diocese to its responsibility to them. The Bishop interested Miss Helen V. Owen of St. John's York, in the program and, as a result, Young People's Fellowships flourished throughout the Diocese. Their annual conventions held each June were a high spot on the social calendar. of the young people. The Rev. Arthur G. W. Pfaffko of Blue Ridge Summit brought fame to the Diocese by conceiving and organizing the Pi Alpha Fraternity for Boys. Their secret rites, the summer camps at Pi Alpha House and the religious training saved many a young man for the church. Encouraged by the rapid spread of Pi Alpha, Mr. Pfaffko organized Tau Delta Alpha for girls. By the end of the period, the young people of the Diocese were joining with young people from the neighboring Dioceses of Pittsburgh and Erie in an annual summer conference at Kiski.

The Bishop and the clergy did more than simply "Hold the Fort." The Church of the Transfiguration at Blue Ridge Summit changed its status from organized mission to incorporated parish; new work was undertaken at Hershey; and the work with Episcopal students at Bucknell which had been done sporadically showed promise .of permanence under the enthusiastic leadership of Rev. J Moulton Thomas of Trinity, Williamsport. The Diocese could take pride in the fact that while the population of the area had grown 5.72 percent the membership of the church had increased 9.7 percent.

IV

It is the privilege of the historian to lift events out of their natural sequence and group them so as to bring movements and trends into sharp focus. This can be done only after a considerable lapse of time when it is possible to see something of the significance of events which seem commonplace at the time of their occurrence. Only the historian can spell out the sequence in a way that leads to an inevitable conclusion. During the course of these events, the plot of the tale is not clear and the denouement is in doubt.

For instance, we now know that the United States reached the trough of the depression in 1932 and had begun the slow climb to prosperity before Roosevelt inaugurated the "new deal." The rise of Hitler and Stalin to the historian are certain portents of a second world war, though at the time war did not appear inevitable. It is one of the blessings of Providence, that we do not know what a day may bring forth so that in dark days we can hope for a better to-morrow. We learn to live with misfortune even as a handicapped person makes a good adjustment to his handicap. Hence, in days of destiny, we go about our business much as if the times were normal.

So it was in the Diocese of Harrisburg in days of depression and in times when the ambition of dictators was drawing the world into the most terrible war of history. Sunday after Sunday, through eleven years, the Bishop set out from Harrisburg to make his canonical visit to one or more parishes and missions. This involved much more travel than had been necessary for Bishop Darlington who went into a district and stayed till all the places had been visited no matter how inconvenient the day or the hour for the people. It had usually fallen to the lot of the smaller parishes and missions to have week night Confirmations and in some cases, they were scheduled on a week day afternoon. Bishop Brown felt that, since the Holy Spirit had come upon the Church at Jerusalem on the first day of the week, Sunday was the most fitting day for the service, and insofar as it was humanly possible, he determined that every parish and mission should have this privilege. In the early days of his Episcopate, he contemplated these Sunday visits with enthusiasm. Having been a parish priest for twenty years, it was a pleasant change to face different congregations, to meet new people and to visit in many homes. His sensitive nature responded to the special welcome which each parish had prepared for its Bishop. Yet, before many years, this constant travel became a tedious chore. He confessed as much publicly at the annual Convention of the Young People's Fellowship in Tyrone in 1935. The fact that he continued to make these journeys year after year, even though he was under the constant care of a doctor for a serious heart condition after 1937, without betraying weariness or boredom and always with a well prepared message of hope and encouragement, is ample testimony to his consecration and spiritual stamina. It must have lightened his labors somewhat to record Confirmation classes averaged around 600. It is interesting to note that the largest class numbered 724, which was received for the year 1933, when new hope came to the nation with the decisive attack upon poverty by the Roosevelt administration. Beside these Sunday visits, further travel was demanded when he was called to attend special parish functions, to institute new Rectors, to ordain priests and deacons, and occasionally to conduct the funeral services for priests and prominent laymen.

At home in Harrisburg, there was the usual round of office routine. Vestries came to him with their problems; priests brought him their troubles and discontents; rectors and missionaries left their cures and had to be replaced; young men, believing they had a vocation, sought his counsel; priests brought him eager candidates to be Confirmed in the Chapel of the Holy Spirit; distinguished Churchmen, visiting Harrisburg, had to be entertained. Thus, in extraordinary times, the Bishop went about the ordinary business of the Episcopate.

Even while the nation hovered on the brink of war, the Bishop gave his attention to what he considered an important family matter. The name "Wyatt" was an honored name in his family and he was anxious to share it with all his children and to have it handed on from generation to generation. It occurred to him that this could be done by changing his name to Wyatt-Brown. This would cause no great difficulty since he had been baptized Hunter Wyatt Brown. By

(100)

reviving the name Hunter (which he had not used) he could thenceforth be known as Hunter Wyatt-Brown. He sought the advice of Judge Reese in this matter, and as a result the legal name was changed in the courts of Cumberland County. For a time, the change was the subject of kindly humor in the Diocese but it soon came to be accepted as a matter of course.

The Convention, too, was able to function quite normally during these momentous days. The experiment of meeting in January begun in 1931 had not proved satisfactory; because of adverse weather conditions in the winter, there was a decided falling off in attendance. Accordingly, Convention returned to the spring meeting in 1937. Since the older Archdeaconries were known by the name of their principal city, it was decided to change the name of the Northern Archdeaconry to the Arthdeaconry of Wellsboro in 1935.

In spite of the fact that the nation was moving rapidly toward war in the spring of 1941, the Diocese did not forget that that year marked the tenth anniversary of the Bishop's consecration. To mark this event, a special service was held in Christ Church, Williamsport where Convention was then meeting. It had been planned to have Bishop Abbot of Lexington (who had been the preacher at the Bishop's consecration) preach the sermon, but he was ill and could not attend, so, at the last moment, Canon Atkins spoke the appreciation of the Diocese for ten years of faithful service. At the reception which followed in the parish house Dean Heistand presented him, in the name of the Diocese, with a tray and silver service.

In the following year, the Diocese undertook two experiments, both of which proved to be shortlived. The first was a brief excursion into the professional field of religious education. Miss Edna Eastwood had been engaged by St. James Church, Lancaster for service as parish Director of Religious Education. Since St. James was willing to share her time with the Diocese she was appointed Educational Missionary and served the Diocese on a part-time basis. Finding she could not stand the constant travel, she resigned after about half a year and her successor was never appointed.

The other experiment was the adoption of the Hare Ballot. Anyone who has been an attendant at a Diocesan Convention knows that one of the most tedious activities is the balloting for the various offices. In years when delegates to General Convention were chosen, this process could become quite time consuming since it usually required many ballots to secure an election. By permitting delegates to indicate several choices in the order of preference the Hare Ballot would assure an election with a single ballot. Because of the complication involved and the difficulty of tabulation, the scheme met with opposition, and in 1946 Convention gave it up.

The period saw the passing of "the Old Guard." First to go was General Clement, who died on September 9, 1934. He had had such a long and close association with the Diocese and the Church at large, that it is worth reprinting the list of his achievements as set forth in a resolution published in the Journal of 1935:

"Whereas, on September 9, 1934, in his 79th year, General Charles M. Clement, Lawyer, soldier, citizen, churchman, answered the Divine summons and the Diocese of Harrisburg was deprived of an able and consecrated leader.

"Therefore be it resolved, that this Convention adopt the following memorial:

"General Clement for many years rendered conspicuous service in the Diocese of Central Pennsylvania, of which at the time of the division he was Secretary. At the request of Bishop Talbot, he issued the call for, and later as Secretary pro-tem convened, the Primary Convention of the Diocese of Harrisburg held in St. James Church, Lancaster, on November 28, 1904, and at once became a familiar figure in its annual deliberations. He served continuously as Secretary, until in 1923 when he became Chancellor and was also at the time of his death Vice President of the Executive Council.

"General Clement was equally prominent in General Convention, serving as lay deputy eleven times, first for the Diocese of Central Pennsylvania and afterwards of the Diocese of Harrisburg in ten conventions. He was a member of many important committees, including the Committee on Lectionary and the Joint Commission to act with similar Commissions of the Methodist, Presbyterian, and Lutheran Churches in the study of matters of Christian morality,

(102)

looking toward organized unity. A memorial presented to General Convention at Atlantic City was unanimously adopted by a rising vote and deputies from the Diocese received many personal expressions of regret and sympathy.

"Busily engaged in the work of his profession and the duties of a soldier and citizen, he nevertheless gave unstintingly of his time and rich legal lore to the consideration of all parish, Diocesan and general church problems and maintained throughout his long life a vital concern for the cause of Christian missions.

"Although possessing the soldier's directness of speech and brusqueness of manner, General Clement was singularly warm and tender-hearted. He loved his fellow men in all walks of life and his circle of friends was large in number and varied in character.

"Grateful for his devotion to the Church and for the example of his noble Christian manhood, we record with sorrow his passing from the Church Militant, as we mourn the loss of his goodly fellowship and wise counsel."

No one could take the General's place, but the position of Chancellor had to be filled, and to this office Convention elected Mr. A. W. Duy of Bloomsburg. He held this position until his death and was succeeded by Mr. Charles L. Miller of Lancaster in 1941.

The year 1934 saw the loss of another familiar figure, the Reverend Lewis Nichols, Rector of St. Paul's, Lock Haven. He had been prominent in the Diocese since its beginning; had served for many years as Archdeacon of Williamsport; had been a close friend of Bishop Darlington and had accompanied him on his trip abroad in 1925. As President of the Standing Committee, he had presided at the conventions which had elected the Diocese's second Bishop. He was so highly regarded by his brethren that he was placed in nomination to succeed Bishop Darlington. After forty years at Lock Haven, he felt that the parish needed younger direction and that he needed lighter work. Accordingly, he resigned to accept a call to be assistant at Trinity Church, New York City.

The next year, the Diocese lost its Treasurer in the death of Mr. Richard M. H. Wharton. Of him, Bishop Brown said in his address to the Convention of 1936:

"On August 4, 1935, in the city of New York, Richard M. H. Wharton suddenly died of heart failure. Mr. Wharton had been Treasurer of the Diocese for fifteen years. He also occupied other important offices more or less contingent upon the Treasurership, in the Incorporated Trustees, the Church Pension Fund, the Committees of Budget and Finance. Anywhere we turn, the face of this devoted servant of Holy Church is missed. Faithful, efficient, kindly to those distressed, generous to those in need. Mr. Wharton deserves our tribute of gratitude and affection. To us clergy and our families, he was a true and loyal friend, and upon us the burden of loss is heavy indeed. Mr. Wharton bequeathed $5,000 to the Diocesan Endowment Fund. The interest on this bequest will relieve every parish and mission just so far on its assignment for the support of the Diocese. May God raise up among us such benefactors, for our Diocesan Endowment is smaller than perhaps that of any Diocese of the Church of approximately the same number of communicants."

The same year saw the retirement of the Venerable Franklin T. Eastmant as Archdeacon of Altoona. His retirement was sorely felt in his Archdeaconry, for he had been Altoona's only Archdeacon. It would have been natural for him to resign when he retired as Rector of St. Paul's, Philipsburg, but his brethren felt that he should continue to be their leader. By 1935, however, he felt that his advanced years entitled him to a rest. As a parish priest he had served with distinction, and as Archdeacon he had acted with patience and wisdom. The beautiful churches at Lewistown and Philipsburg are enduring monuments to his energy and foresight. After his retirement as Rector of St. Paul's he continued to live in Philipsburg till his death in 1940. The parish elected him Rector Emeritus and he discharged this office with rare tact., never interfering with the work of his successors but always stood ready to give them his godly counsel. Few men more richly deserved the title which goes with the office of Archdeacon.

On May 1, 1939, Dr. Clifford Gray Twombly preached his last sermon as Rector of St. James, Lancaster. He had been Rector of that parish for 32 years and had been prominent in the affairs of the Diocese throughout its history. Taking cognizance of his retirement, Bishop Brown spoke of him thus in his Convention Address of 1939.

"Dr. Twombly spent 32 years in St. James Church, Lancaster. He is best known outside his parish as a stern prophet of rigid righteousness, but within his fold he is known as a faithful parish visitor in the home of his people, rich and poor alike. Against such a ministry as his, pride and prejudice and indifference gradually disintegrate and disappear."

The years saw other changes in leadership. Except at the Church of the Transfiguration, Blue Ridge Summit, and St. John's, York, all the churches had one or more new Rectors. Lock Haven had a succession of Rectors after the resignation of Mr. Nichols; Francis D. Daley, Strafford C. Jones, William J. Watts, Blake B. Hammond and F. Graham Luckenbill.

Dean Treder resigned from the Cathedral in 1933 and was succeeded by the Rev. J. Thomas Heistand, who had been called from Bloomsburg. The Rev. Richard Allen Hatch was succeeded at St. Luke's, Altoona, by the Rev. Francis D. Daley, who went to Pine Bluff, Arkansas, in 1940. St. Luke's then called the Rev. John R. Leatherbury from Sparrow's Point, Maryland.

On the resignation of the Rev. Charles E. McCoy, Trinity Williamsport, called the Rev. J. Moulton Thomas from Hancock, Maryland. When Canon Bennett was elected Dean of the Cathedral in Wilmington, Christ Church, Williamsport, called the Rev. Ernest E. Piper who had been an assistant at St. Bartholomew's, New York. After a short tenure, he accepted a call to Detroit and was succeeded at Williamsport by the Rev. Stuart F. Gast.

At Bloomsburg, the Rev. Stuart F. Gast succeeded the Rev. J. Thomas Heistand; when he was called to Williamsport, he was followed by the Rev. Earl M. Honaman who had been Rector of St. Andrew's, Harrisburg. When Mr. Honaman entered militory service, the Rev. Willis R. Doyle served briefly as locum tenens to be followed by the Rev. William J. Watts who had been called from St. Luke's, Mount Joy.

At. St. John's, Lancaster, the Rev. Frederick P. Houghton was succeeded by Rev. John W. Mulder. When he took a parish in Kentucky in 1936, St. John's called the Rev. Heber W. Becker from Christ Church, Danville. Dr. Twombly's successor at St. James, was the Rev. Robert C. Batchelder. At St. Paul's, Philipsburg, the Rev. Charles E. Knickle was succeeded by the Rev. Lewis D. Gotschall who had been called from Berwick; when he left for California, the parish called the Rev. William Lickfield from Westfield.

At Lewistown, the Rev. Thomas Worrall was succeeded by the Rev. Myles A. Vollmer; and at Sunbury, Rev. Anthony G. Van Elden was succeeded by the Rev. Wayne N. Wagonseller. When the Rev. Stuart Gast was called to Bloomsburg, St. John's, Bellefonte, had as its Rectors the Rev. Robert D. Sudlow, Rev. Samuel Sayre, Rev. Robert N. Thomas, 3rd, the Rev. Herbert Koepp-Baker and the Rev. Francis P. Davis.

All the Archdeaconries had changes in leadership. In the Archdeaconry of Wellsboro, Archdeacon Schmaus was succeeded by the Rev. Harry H. Gillies. On his tragic death, the Rev. J. Perry Cox became Archdeacon. Archdeacon Cox remained in the Diocese but a short time and he was succeeded as Archdeacon by the Rev. John G. Hilton.

In the Archdeaconry of Williamsport, Archdeacon McCoy was succeeded by the Rev. Robert T. McCutcheon. When he left Shamokin to become Chaplain at Mount Alto Sanatorium, he was succeeded by the Rev. Anthony G. Van Elden. When he left Sunbury to become Vicar of St. Mary's, Waynesboro, and Prince of Peace, Gettysburg, his place was taken by the Rev. Squire B. Schofield, Rector of Christ Church, Danville.

In Harrisburg, the Rev. W. Josselyn Reed succeeded Archdeacon Hughes in 1937. When he entered the military service, he was succeeded by the Rev. William J. Watts who was soon called to Bloomsburg. He was succeeded by the Rev. Donald C. Means, who kept the post until he entered military service, when Rev. Robert T. McCutcheon was named Archdeacon of Harrisburg.

On the retirement of Archdeacon Eastmant, the Rev. William T. Sherwood became Archdeacon of Altoona. When he left the Diocese to take a parish in Brownsville, Texas, the Rev. F. William Lickfield was made Archdeacon.

These changes in leadership necessitated some reallignment of the Cathedral Canons—only Canons Atkins and French remained constant throughout the period. Canon Hatch was replaced by the Rev. L. D. Gotschall and he in turn by the Rev. Edward M. Frear, Vicar of St. Andrew's, State College. Rev. Stuart F. Gast replaced Canon Bennett and the Rev. Heber W. Becker replaced Canon Twombly.

We have already noted the fact that the Bishop was under doctor's care after 1937. The duties of his office became so burdensome that he asked the Convention of 1941 to grant him a six-months' leave of absence in the hope that a complete rest would restore him to health. This request, of course, was granted, and on July 28, he turned over the Ecclestical Authority to the Standing Committee. Group Confirmations were held at various centers during the fall and winter with the assistance of Bishops Sterrett of Bethlehem, Ward of Erie and Zeigler of Wyoming. Bishop Ward also graciously offered his service for the ordination of several candidates for Holy Orders.

When the Bishop returned to the Diocese in March, 1942, he seemed much improved in health, but the improvement was only temporary. He was ill again during the summer and by the following spring he was persuaded to take his doctor's advice and retire on disability. In order that his going might affect the Diocese as little as possible, he asked the Convention of 1943 to elect a Bishop Coadjutor to whom he promised to surrender all salary and authority as soon as he should be consecrated.

Although the prospect of an untimely retirement must have been very distressing, he sought to hide his feelings from his Diocese. As he walked down Front Street to the Cathedral on Convention Day, and saw clergy and laity forgathered outside as was the custom, he observed with a smile: "Well, the cohorts are gathered." He was able to preside over the Convention with his usual poise even through the trying moments when his successor was being elected. Only in the course of his convention address did he reveal his deep feeling. There were tears in many eyes as the delegates heard him say:

> "Since 1937, we have been under a physician's care. During the first eleven years of our Episcopate only two scheduled services for Confirmation were omitted or postponed by the Bishop for any cause whatsoever. But many of these

visitations were made in weather when travel was well nigh impossible and ofttimes when our physical condition made the long trips almost unbearable. Of late the strain has become greater.

"As you know, therefore, under the advice of our physician we gave consent for the election of a Bishop Coadjutor. The ground upon which the consent was based was physical infirmity, and not the extent of territory. Since the question of the election of a Bishop Coadjutor was placed before the clergy of the Diocese and their parishes and missions we have suffered certain functional attacks of the heart. These attacks are due to nervous strain and arterio-sclerosis. They are physically weakening and mentally disconcerting while they last.

"At last, to our infinite regret, it has become more and more evident that we can no longer bear the strain and responsibility of the active Episcopate. Upon the urgent advce of Dr. Ernest S. Gross of the John Hopkins Hospital Staff, Baltimore, Maryland, and with the approval of the Medical Board of the Church Pension Fund, we have sent to the Presiding Bishop of the Church our resignation as Bishop of Harrisburg, to be presented by him to the House of Bishops when it convenes on October 2, 1943.

"Therefore, if you proceed to an election today, as we earnestly advise you to do, you will be electing a Bishop Coadjutor who will become the Bishop of the Diocese as soon as our retirement is made effective by the House of Bishops in General Convention assembled.

"Furthermore, we assure you that on the day of the Consecration of the Bishop Coadjutor, the Bishop of the Diocese will relinquish to him all jurisdiction, and at the same time relinquish to him all salary accruing to the Episcopate. You will in effect, therefore, be electing today our successor in office.

"We dare not try to express to you all that we feel at this time. We of course hoped to be able to continue our work as Bishop until the retirement age of 68. We looked forward to eight more years of blessed and devoted companion-

(108)

ship with our clergy and our people, but this was not God's will for us, and we accept His Will without complaint.

"The twelve years since our consecration in St. Stephen's Cathedral on May 1, 1931, have been years of joyous service and friendly associaton. We are sure that no Bishop in the Church has a more loyal company of diocesan priests than those we have gradually gathered around us in the Diocese of Harrisburg. We can truthfully say that we love each and every one of our clergy as though he was a real son. Whatever faults we have committed and whatever erroneous judgments we have made in regard to our clergy have been of the head and never of the heart. We have consistently endeavored to promote priests within the Diocese to posts of greater responsiblity and to inculcate among them a desire in honor to prefer one another. The laity of the Diocese also have co-operated with the Bishap in such a way that we shall be able to promise our successor an effective and happy Episcopate.

"In our resignation to the Presiding Bishop we expressed our thanks to God for having called us to be the spiritual leader of 'The devoted clergy and responsive laymen of one of the most loyal dioceses in the American Church.' And this Thanksgiving is genuine and unstinted. These twelve years will ever be remembered reverently and happily by us for they are the crown and climax of the 42 years in which we have preached the Gospel of Our Blessed Lord. Our consoling thought is that as long as we live our title will still be 'The Retired Bishop of Harrisburg.' In General Convention, should we be able to attend, that will be our title. Within the Diocese of Harrisburg that will be our title—'the Retired Bishop of Harrisburg,' but still a Bishop of the Church, and connected by ties which can never be severed with the Diocese of Harrisburg. And the best of this consoling thought is that our legal and canonical residence will still be within the confines of the Diocese we love.

"Our successor need never fear interference on our part. But our prayers will be ever for him in his work, and our service, limited though it may be, will be ever at his call.

"And so, my brethren, this is not farewell. It is only the announcement of a change in our canonical relationship which can never affect our personal relationship in Christ Jesus our Lord."

Later in the Convention, Canon Atkins spoke the mind of the Diocese in these words of loving tribute:

"Dear Bishop Wyatt-Brown, our prayers and good wishes follow you. We rejoice that you have chosen to dwell among us, an honored and beloved member of our household of faith. Happy are we in the knowledge that we shall see your face again. Released from the heavy responsibilities of your high and Holy Office restored, refreshed and renewed, we know that you will find opportunity for further service, as your strength permits. We commend you to the care of our loving Lord, Whom so tenderly, you have revealed to us. Who has led you all the way. May the Holy Spirit abide with you always, even to the glorious and triumphant fulfillment."

Chapter Five

HARRISBURG CALLS A NATIVE SON

I

The grief caused by the news of Bishop Wyatt-Brown's retirement was somewhat mitigated by the excitement involved in the choice of his successor. Speculation as to the person upon whom the mantle would fall was universal in the Diocese in the days before the Convention. In general the clergy took the lead in bringing candidates forward and the laity followed their leadership, believing that they were not qualified to judge since they did not have the necessary information. The Diocese was divided upon the question as to whether the Bishop should be selected from within or without the Diocese. There was a feeling that there were men within the Diocese who had experience and qualifications to be the Chief Pastor; moreover, it was pointed out that such a man would have an intimate knowledge of conditions which would be an invaluable asset. On the other hand, some felt that while there might be men who could qualify, they would be handicapped by their intimacy with the Diocese and their intimate associaton with those whom they would be called upon to lead. Further, being so close to the situation, a local man could not judge as objectively as a man who came to the Diocese from the outside.

Local aspirants were not lacking and it was understood that some of them would be placed in nomination. Some of them had won considerable support in the Diocese by Convention time while others had only the support of their own parish and that of their immediate neighbors. Knowing the sentiment for a man from outside the Diocess, a Committee had been appointed to canvass the field and present to the Convention available men with a brief account of their qualifications without making any specific recommendations. Parties had crystallized by Convention time and the excitement was such that the election of delegates to General Convention (which was also on the agenda for the Convention) was largely disregarded.

When Convention opened, a motion was made to suspend the Rules of Order so as to permit the making of nominations for Bishop Coadjutor during the first session in order that balloting might begin that night. This was deemed necessary in order that Convention might give its major attention on the second day to the election of delegates to General Convention.

Canon Atkins, acting for the committee to present available candidates, placed the following names before the Convention: Rev. Samuel Whitney Hale, Rector of the Church of the Advent, Boston; The Very Rev. Roscoe T. Foust, Dean of the Pro Cathedral of the Nativity, Bethlehem; Rev. Don Frank Fenn, Rector of St. Michael and All Angels, Baltimore; Rev. Frank D. Gifford, Mamaroneck, New York; The Very Rev. Harry Austin Pardue, Dean of St. Paul's Cathedral, Buffalo; Rev. Elwood Lindsey Haines of Louisville; Rev. Richard F. Loring, Rector of St. David's Church, Baltimore; Rev. C. Avery Mason of New York City who had been working with the Forward Movement Commission; Rev. Frederick L. Barry of Evanston, Illinois; and the Rev. A. Appleton Packard of West Park, New York, a member of the Order of the Holy Cross.

From within the Diocese the following men were placed in nomination: Rev. Paul S. Atkins of Christ Church, Williamsport, The Very Rev. J. Thomas Heistand, Dean of St. Stephen's Cathedral, Harrisburg; Rev. W. Josselyn Reed, in Military Service; Rev. John R. Leatherbury, Rector of St. Luke's Church, Altoona; and the Rev. Arthur G. W. Pfaffko, Rector of the Church of the Transfiguration, Blue Ridge Summit.

It was plain to those who listened to the talk among the delegates between the afternoon and evening session, that the party that favored a local man had united in support of Dean Heistand, while those who favored electing an outsider would support the Rev. Don Frank Fenn. The relative strength of the two parties was evident in the result of the first ballot. There were, of course, many complimentary votes cast, but the result showed Dean Heistand definitely in the lead. On the second ballot, he was elected by the laity and on the third, he received a majority in both orders and was declared elected. The election was over before ten o'clock—a remarkable achievement in view of the previous struggles to elect a Bishop.

During the course of the election, Bishop Wyatt-Brown, of course, maintained a strict neutrality, but when it was over his pleasure at the result was unmistakable. "The Diocese has come of age," he shouted over the enthusiasm which was manifest in the Convention when the result was announced. When order was restored, the Bishop-Elect made a modest acceptance speech, Convention rose and sang the Doxology and adjourned in the spirit of harmony and thankfulness. While the delegates dispersed to hotel rooms to hold a post mortem over the outcome, the Bishop-Elect retired to the Deanery where, after sending his family out, he faced the responsibilities and challenges of his office alone with God.

It was a foregone conclusion that the third Bishop of Harrisburg would be the Right Reverend John Thomas Heistand, but there were certain formalities that had to be observed before he could be Consecrated. Every Bishop and every Standing Committee in the Church had to be notified of the election and their consent asked. Unless a majority of the Bishops and a majority of the Standing Committees consented to it, the election would not be valid. By midsummer, the necessary consents had been obtained and plans were set afoot for the Consecration. After consulting with the Presiding Bishop, Wednesday, September 15, was set as the date, and most appropriately, the Cathedral was to be scene of the solemn ceremony.

Consecration Day could not have been finer. There was a slight nip in the air in the morning which gave promise of the autumn to come, but by mid-morning, the sun shone warm in a sky of azure. From all parts of the Diocese, people set out for Harrisburg, some to see a ceremony repeated which they had taken part in a dozen years before, and others to have a new experience, but all eager to clasp the hand of their new Bishop and pledge to him their loyalty and support.

Since we described the Consecration of Bishop Wyatt-Brown in some detail, there is need here only to mention the names of those who took part in the service of Consecraton for Bishop Heistand. The Master of Ceremonies was the Rev. Canon Heber W. Becker and his assistant was the Rev. Charles P. James. The Marshalls of the Procession which moved into the Church to the singing of "Ancient of Days" and "O 'Twas a Joyful Sound to Hear" were: Rev. Canon Stuart F. Gast, Rev. J. Moulton Thomas, Rev. John R. Leatherbuy, Rev. Wayne M. Wagenseller, Rev. Robert C. Batchelder and the Venerable Robert T. McCutcheon.

The celebrant at the Holy Communion, and the Consecrator, was the Rt. Rev. Henry St. George Tucker, Presiding Bishop of the

(113)

Church; the Co-Consecrators were the Rt. Rev. Frank W. Sterrett, Bishop of Bethlehem and the Rt. Rev. Hunter Wyatt-Brown, who read the Epistle and Gospel respectively; the sermon was preached by the Rt. Rev. Noble C. Powell, Bishop of Maryland; Dean Heistand, who was attended by Rev. Paul S. Atkins and Rev. Harry D. Viets, was presented to the Presiding Bishop for Consecration by the Rt. Rev. William McClelland, Bishop of Easton, and the Rt. Rev. Wallace J. Gardner, Bishop of New Jersey.

The Certificate of Election was read by Mr. Lesley McCreath; the Canonical Testimonial by Mr. Charles L. Miller; the Certificate of Ordination by the Rev. Canon Clifford W. French; the Consents of the Standing Committees of the Church by Mr. John I. Hartman; and the Consents of the Bishops of the Church by the Rt. Rev. Alexander Mann, Bishop of Pittsburgh. The Rt. Rev. Oliver J. Hart, Bishop of Pennsylvania, read the Litany. Those who witnessed the solemn procession, the presentation of the Bishop-Elect, and the act of Consecration had an experience which they would never forget.

Following the service, a luncheon was given the new Bishop and his family and those who had taken part in the services. Meanwhile, a buffet luncheon was served to all who had attended the service. As the people of the Diocese dispersed to their homes, the glory of the beautiful day seemed a visible evidence of the blessing of God upon the Diocese and an assurance that all was well.

II

Bishop Heistand was truly a native son of the Diocese. Born in Lancaster County in 1895, he grew up as a member of St. John's parish in Lancaster. He was licensed as a Lay Reader there in 1916 and shortly thereafter was made a Postulant for Holy Orders. The war interrupted his studies at the General Theological Seminary, for he felt impelled to join the young men who were engaged in a crusade for freedom. During the war, he served in France where he was severely gassed. At the end of the war, he returned to General but did not stay to graduate.

On being ordained to the Diaconate, he was sent as a missionary to the hard coal regions where his circuit included the Church of the

Ascension, Kulpmont; St. Nathaniel's, Natalie; and the Church of the Holy Trinity at Centralia. After two years, he was transferred to Milton. While serving there, he lived at Lewisburg where he began a work among the Episcopal students at Bucknell. From Milton, he was called to Bloomsburg and his missionary days were over. He was Rector of St. Paul's for eight years till he was called to succeed Dean Treder at St. Stephen's Cathedral.

His influence in the Diocese increased with his advancement. He served on various boards and commissions and at the time of his election, was Secretary of the Standing Committee and Chairman of the Youth Commission. Living close to Bishop Wyatt-Brown, he became his counsellor and confidante.

The Bishop brought to the Diocese a rich fund of experience. From personal knowledge, he could sympathize with the young missionary who was set down in a bleak village deprived of the comforts and cultural advantages to which he was accustomed. He knew how easily such a young man could be discouraged and disillusioned when his enthusiasm was met by conservatism and indifference. He knew the sacrifices young wives had to make as they made shift to live in rectories sometimes so large that they could neither furnish nor heat them and sometimes so small that anything approaching gracious living was impossible. He knew the ingenuity that was necessary to stretch the inadequate salary of the missionary to meet the minimum demands of a decent standard of living. He knew the problems of the youngster who thinks home intolerable and decides to run away; of the college student who expresses his independence by wild escapades or by mouthing words of agnosticism which he believes gives him a sophisticated air. He knew parish life as it is lived in the small Pennsylvana town and that of a Dean in a city Cathedral. He had struggled with obstinate Vestries, he had cajoled people to teach in his Church School, he had worked with his people to raise funds for various causes, he had had his troubles with organizations where petty jealousy and selfishness threatened the peace of the parish.

He knew, too, the joys of the Priesthood. In every place he served, he had friends who had become dear through the sharing of joy and sorrow. He had pronounced the blessing of the Church upon young people who had grown up under his ministry and who stood before him at the Altar to plight their troth each to the other. He had officiated at the Font as these young people brought their children to Holy Baptism. Sunday after Sunday, he had the privilege of giving his people the Blessed Sacrament and standing in his pulpit to speak to them in God's name. He had seen tense faces relax as he assured those who came with an unquiet conscience of God's complete forgiveness. He had spoken words of comfort to those whose bereavement threatened them with despair. He had learned to live constantly under the eye of his Bishop.

Moreover, he knew the temper of the people of central Pennsylvania. He knew their conservatism, their economic insecurity, their suspicion of a ritualistic church. In short, he knew what it meant to live and work in the Diocese of Harrisburg.

In his close relations with Bishop Wyatt-Brown, he had a rare opportunity to become acquainted with the problems which every Bishop must face. He knew of the wearisome journeys, the dissatisfactions of the clergy, the complaints of unsympathetic Vestries, and the gruelling schedule of office routine. As the Bishop's health declined, he sought to relieve him of his burdens and in so doing, learned the nature and problems of the Episcopate almost at first hand.

The new Bishop was a simple man. He disliked sham and pretense and all the trappings of office. As parish priest, he was a friend to high and low. The warmth of his personality drew people to him and inspired their confidence. He was quick to sense and respond to people's moods and his sympathetic nature often led him to make promises beyond his power to fulfill. He was easily approached both by the people of his parish and by the people of the town where he happened to live. In his preaching, his life spoke more eloquently than his words. The high esteem in which he was held in Harrisburg is seen in the fact that the city was as much interested in his election as was his most ardent partisan.

The Episcopate did not spoil this simplicity. At his consecration, he insisted on a simple service. Upon his election, he announced that he would not live at Bishopscourt with its baronial hall, private chapel and all that was reminiscent of the palaces of the English prelates. He wanted a home in which he and his family could live a normal American family life, where friends could call as in an ordinary home and where he could be a good neighbor among average people. Accordingly, Bishopscourt was sold, and a new Episcopal residence purchased at 2405 North Front Street. He continued to have an easy comraderie with those who for so long had been his brothers; he never allowed his office to create a gulf between himself and them. When he visited parishes for Confirmation, he would have no Bishop's Chair brought forward, but stood simply at the Altar rail to lay his hands on those who were presented to him—in so doing, he felt that he was really following the example of the blessed Apostles. He resisted all efforts to put him in cope and mitre. In some respects, he bent over backwards to minimize his office in the eyes of clergy and laity, for he did not wish his personality as a man to be obscured by his high office.

He did not have the breadth of interests of Bishop Darlington nor the benevolent paternalism of Bishop Wyatt-Brown. He was neither artist, poet, nor musician, he did not know the great of the land nor the kings of the earth. He was simply a son of Lancaster County called to be Chief Shepherd of a Diocese. He shared the pleasures of ordinary people. In the spring he loved to sit by a trout stream and try to lure the speckled beauties and in the fall he knew the joys of the chase. As a young man, he had played baseball with more than the skill of an amateur and he maintained his interest in the game with advancing years. While he knew the ways of the world, he was not worldly. No one could doubt either his sincerity or his religious zeal.

All this experience and all these qualities he brought to his office, and he brought something more. He knew the Diocese from the standpoint of the clergy. In many a room filled with smoke he had joined his brothers in speaking their minds freely as only the clergy can when they foregather. From these meetings he knew of situations and jealousies about which a Bishop seldom learns. There were problems in the Diocese which the previous Bishops could not or would not see which cried for solution. He was aware of cleavages which could be concealed during a Bishop's visitation but which if allowed to widen, would bode no good for the Diocese.

In his first Convention address, he set the tone of his administration as he set before the delegates his conception of the Church and his personality shines through the words.

(117)

"As I see it, the Church is at one and the same time a Family, wherein we realize our individual worth, a School in which we are instructed in the eternal truths of our holy religion, a Hospital to which we come for repair and medicine for our broken souls and bodies, an Army in which we take our places in the ranks to fight against sin, the world and the devil, and to continue Christ's faithful soldiers therein unto our life's end.

"Thinking, then of the Church in those four aspects, we come to this our first Convention as a Father of a Family, a Teacher whose duty it is to instruct in love, a Cure or Doctor of souls, and a militant Leader calling upon his command for action."

Commenting on a situation in the Diocese which had been largely ignored by his predecessors, he expressed sentiments which he was to repeat again and again in the course of the next ten years. Because his critics read into his words more than was in his mind, misunderstandings developed in the Diocese which laid a heavy burden upon the Bishop's heart. It is well, therefore, to have the Bishop's attitude clearly stated in order to appreciate his deep concern for the welfare of the Diocese of which he was the Father in God:

"Within the fabric of any parish which is functioning as our Blessed Lord intends it to function much thought is given to the services of the Church. It is here we come to receive refreshment and strength, as well as to offer praise and adoration to Almighty God. It is alarming then to find unhappy divisions in our parishes, caused by that which is most popularly referred to as a difference in Churchmanship, which really should be defined as a difference in ceremonialism. For it is not a difference in our beliefs as to the great doctrines of the Church, but rather in the ceremonial acts through which we express those doctrines. It is this difference in ceremonial which causes most of the difficulties which seriously hinder the real work of the Church and the purpose for which it exists, the winning of souls for the Kingdom of God.

"In calling your attention to these unhappy divisions, I do so not as a critic, nor do I for one moment claim to be

(118)

an authority in the field of liturgics. However, as your Bishop, I would feel that I had failed in my responsibility were I not to plead with you, both clergy and laity, to exercise that charity which is the mark of a true Christian in your relations with each other. It has been my observation that with the exercise of tolerance, the consideration of others, and a willingness to reason together, many of our differences would be resolved, and a spirit of harmony and peace would prevail within the brotherhood.

"Thus our Church would radiate an atmosphere of joy and peace, which is so needed by each of us in these days of war with its cruelty and hatred, its strains and stress upon our souls. The dominant note of the early Church was this joy that came through the fellowship with each other in the brotherhood of a common cause, and in the close communion of the fellowship with their risen Lord. It is my honest conviction that as we recapture this spirit of joy in the brotherhood the Church will once again attract many souls who are seeking an answer to the meaning of life, which can only be given by that which has been defined as the extension of the Incarnation: the One, Holy, Catholic and Apostolic Church.

" 'Like a mighty army moves the Church of God.' So we sing in one of the greatest hymns of the Christian Church. That we have a militant leader is abundantly proven in the accounts of his life and teachings as recorded in the Gospel story. From the days of his temptation in the wilderness until his last expiring breath upon the cross the life of our Blessed Lord was a steadfast refusal to compromise with sin and all the ugly evils that follow in its train, evils that result in many of the ills that prevail in our world today. His method was one of attack, a fearless facing up to anything that was contrary to the revealed Will of his Father. I believe the Church, if it is true to its Master, must do likewise, or it will be cast aside, much as that Church which our Lord found in the world of his days on earth was cast aside.

. . . .

"It is still true—'if a man lose his life for my sake and

(119)

the Gospel, he shall find it.' With the promise of our risen Lord—'Lo, I am with you alway even unto the end of the world'—ringing in our hearts and minds, let us take up our work with joyful hearts and willing hands."

Such was the man who was consecrated Bishop Coadjutor on September 15, 1943, and such the man who upon the retirement of Bishop Wyatt-Brown the following October 4 became the third Bishop of Harrisburg.

III

The first problem which the Bishop tackled after he became the Diocesan was the plight of his missionary clergy and the state of the missions in the Diocese. From the beginning of its history, the Diocese had experienced great difficulty in raising enough money to maintain its missions and to pay its quota to the national Church. There were opportunities for the Church in various communities, for example Hershey and Hanover, which could not be taken advantage of because no funds were available. It was hoped through the adoption of the Hartman Plan, to encourage missionary giving by putting it on a more voluntary basis, but the number of parishes willing to accept a normal quota was disappointingly small. Moreover, after 1939, the country had begun to climb the inflation spiral. Yet people continued to give to the Church as if the pre-war price level still prevailed. The Bishop felt that if the Diocese was to be true to its trust, something must be done and at once.

The root of the trouble, of course, was parochialism. A symptom of the attitude is indicated by the misinterpretation of the letters IP after the name of a parish in the Journal; for most people, those letters stood for "Independent Parish." This feeling of independence was accentuated by the fact that most churches were isolated, for it was only at such times as the annual Convention and the annual meeting of the Woman's Auxiliary that the people of the Diocese got together. Even then, the group that knew each other well was small. The problems of the parish loomed so large that the problems of the Diocese and the national Church seemed insignificant by comparison. Money was hard to come by in the parish and those who had earned it were reluctant to see it go out of the parish. The Rectors

(120)

did not usually share this attitude, but they became discouraged in trying to combat parochial inertia and after a time their vision faded.

The Bishop had enough confidence in his people to believe that the situation could be corrected if the people knew the facts; he further believed that they would respond to his personal appeal. So, in the spirit of the "fireside chat" which President Roosevelt had been using so effectively to bring national problems home to the people, the Bishop arranged regional Vestry meetings throughout the Diocese. All the members of the Vestries in a particular area and the Rectors of the parishes which they represented were invited to be the Bishop's guests at dinner. During the fellowship of the meal, parochial leaders became better acquainted and at its close the Bishop presented the Field Work picture and asked the Vestries to confer with their Rectors then and there and report to him what quota they would assume for the coming year, stressing the importance of each parish and mission accepting at least a normal quota. To encourage them to do this, he assured delinquent parishes that he would recommend that they be exonerated from all arrearages owing to the Diocese so that they could start with a clean slate. The result of these meetings was most gratifying, and the Bishop confessed that he felt humbled in the face of the generous response to his appeal.

The same plan was followed a year later and put in charge of the Department of Promotion. The Department did an excellent job, but the novelty had worn off and the strain to keep up with inflation seemed so great that some parishes and missions slipped back into their old ways. That this problem was not confined to the Diocese of Harrisburg is indicated by the fact that the National Council began holding training schools for the Department of Promotion hoping by this means to stimulate missionary giving throughout the Church so that the larger demands growing out of post-war needs and the new program of Christian education might be met. The Diocese co-operated in this training program and thus had men available either to conduct regional Vestry meetings or to go into a parish to inspire congregations before they undertook their Every Member Canvass. But the results were often disappointing. Men were increasingly reluctant to take the time to attend the regional Vestry meeting and Vestries felt they did not need outside help with their canvass. We must not give the impression that there has not been a great increase in Field Work giving since 1943, but the demands have

(121)

outstripped the gifts and the Field Work budget has been rarely subscribed. On the occasion when the budget was in balance, it was not due to increased giving but to the fact that certain money allocated for missionary salaries was unused due to vacancies in the mission field.

There has been some dissatisfaction with the Hartman Plan since quotas are based on average parish expenses during the preceding three years. It is contended that this plan favors the parishes which keep their expenses down and penalizes those which raise the salary of their Rector and make needed parish improvements. Moreover, it has been pointed out, that if the quota is figured on a per capita basis, the larger parishes seemed to have a distinct advantage. As a result of this thinking, a committee was appointed to study the possibility of determining quotas on a communicant basis and to make the Field Work Fund a charge upon the parish like the Diocesan assessment. After a careful study of this suggestion, the committee concluded that such a plan would not be in accord with the principle of ability to pay and it would violate the principle that contributions to missions are essentially a voluntary gift. It therefore recommended that the Diocese continue to operate under the Hartman Plan.

At the spring meeting of the Executive Council in 1954, the Bishop stated that the time had come to face realistically the problem of the unbalanced Field Work budget. He pointed out that the same parishes and missions were failing year after year to meet their obligations, and in some instances, these places were receiving generous Diocesan aid. He called for a reappraisal of the work being done by the missionaries and a critical study of the opportunities open to the church in places which were beng aided by the Diocese. He felt, too, that further study should be given to the methods of determining Field Work quotas. Moved by the Bishop's earnest appeal, the Department of Promotion has taken the matter under advisement and has promised to report a plan which will correct the situation. It will be left to those who lead the Diocese in its second half century to see if they can devise a scheme of education and assessment which will help the Diocese to continue more nearly meeting its obligations to the people of the territory within its limits.

Yet, the picture is not all dark. Through the constant insistence of the Bishop, salaries of missionaries have been raised substantially so that the minimum salary of $3,000 is in force in almost every instance. A canon was adopted fixing the minimum salary of a Rector of a parish at $3,300. Yet, this improvement is deceptive, for the value of the dollar has shrunk so low that the clergy find themselves but little better off than they were when the minimum salary was $1,800.

Another fiscal problem with which the Bishop was deeply concerned was the Diocesan endowment. While Dean of the Cathedral, he was leader in the movement to bring this problem home to the Diocese and to devise ways in which the fund could be increased without placing an undue burden upon the parishes and missions. As Bishop, he felt a personal interest in this matter, and he felt keenly the fact that the Episcopate was a heavy tax upon the Diocese. Acordingly, in 1944, he proposed that on the last Sunday of November each communicant in the Diocese should be asked to contribute at least one dollar to this fund, and that they should continue to make this contribution year after year. Convention adopted this suggestion but provided no means of enforcement other than moral suasion, and, as might be expected, little was accomplished.

The Bishop approached the problem again in 1951 by proposing that the Diocese undertake a campaign for $300,000, one-third to be placed in the Endowment Fund, one-third to be used for forward work in the Diocese, and the rest to be used for the purchase of a conference centre. But the proposal was so coldly received that it was dropped. The approach of the 50th anniversary of the setting apart of the Diocese seemed the opportunity for which the Bishop had been waiting. Sentiment was general that the Diocese ought to undertake something significant in celebration of this event. A committee was appointed in 1952 to give the matter study and report to the Convention of 1953. The committee recommended that the Diocese undertake a campaign for $200,000, one-half of which was to go to the Endowment Fund and one-half to be used for forward work. Convention adopted their recommendation with some enthusiasm.

After consulting with a firm of professional fund raisers, the committee was convinced that it had set its sights too low. It was pointed out that to raise the Endowment Fund by only $100,000 would not greatly strengthen the financial position of the Episcopate and a fund of $100,000 would not permit the Diocese to take a very long step forward. Moreover, the cost of raising so small an amount would be disproportionately high. After careful consideration, it was determined to raise the amount to $400,000 and a Special Convention was called to meet on September 22 to ratify the action. Though opinion in the Convention was not unanimous, Convention voted to undertake the larger campaign.

But again the Bishop was doomed to disappointment. There was some dissatisfaction with hiring professional fund raisers; certain parishes felt they could not participate fully in the campaign because they had assumed heavy obligations in making parish improvements; the general Church was launching a campaign for $4,000,000 known as "Builders for Christ" which the Presiding Bishop felt should have priority over any Diocesan effort; and finally, with the Korean War over, the country was entering a period of readjustment which made the economic future difficult to forecast. In view of all this, the Bishop felt that it would be wise not to undertake the campaign. With a heavy heart, he asked the Executive Council to postpone the campaign indefinitely, when it met in December and Council acceded to his wishes. Thus, the problem of the Endowment, which has plagued the Diocese since its founding, is passed on to the leaders of the future.

"The Builders for Christ" campaign was only one of several which the Church called upon the Diocese to share. After the war, the Church undertook what was called "The Reconstruction Advance Campaign." As a result, the Diocese raised $77,000 earmarked for the equipment of St. Luke's Hospital in Shanghai. Cognizant of the suffering caused by the war, the Church launched a three-year campaign known as the Presiding Bishop's Fund for World Relief. The campaign of 1949 was launched in a spectacular way. Known as "One Great Hour of Sharing," the people of the Diocese were urged to attend church services at eleven o'clock when the Presiding Bishop spoke to the whole Church by radio. To facilitate this program, the Presiding Bishop's address was recorded for use in those churches where radio reception was not good. All of these services were very impressive and the resulting canvass was quite satisfactory.

To bring the Episcopal Church to the attention of the public, the National Department of Promotion inaugurated a series of nationwide radio programs known as "Great Scenes from Great Plays."

Through the Episcopal Actors' Guild, these scenes were portrayed in a masterful way and those who listened to the programs were highly entertained and sometimes edified. Opinions differ as to the result. In the Diocese of Harrisburg, Friday night was largely given over to the football games played by local High Schools and it is doubtful whether these programs reached as large an audience as they should. In each area, the local Episcopal Church was mentioned by name and an invitation was extended to visit this church and to write the Rector if interested in receiving more information about the Church. The response to this invitation was disappointing, and the national Church found itself at the end of the 26 weeks with a considerable deficit.

By 1943 the Hymnal: 1940 was ready for distribution. It was received with mingled emotions. Some of the unfamiliar tunes were not popular, the new pointing of the chants met with resistance, and some of the older people missed familiar hymns. However, by 1954, this Hymnal had been generally adopted and, as it became more familiar, its merits were appreciated. By the end of the period under survey, the clergy were becoming interested in the studies made looking to a revision of the Prayer Book, and the proposed service of Holy Communion had been used experimentally at Archdeaconry meetings.

Perhaps the most significant contact of the Diocese with the general Church was in the field of Christian Education. In February 1950, the clergy of the Diocese met in Williamsport with Dr. John Huess, Chairman of the National Department of Christian Education, and received their first briefing on the philosophy underlying the new curriculum being prepared for the Church School and were given some notion of its probable content. This indoctrination was continued at the College of Preachers and at special conferences. During the fall of 1951, members of the Diocesan Department presented a script entitled "Toward Redemptive Life" at regional meetings throughout the Diocese. The books in the Church's Teaching series were read and studied and there was a noticeable increase in interest in adult education. At the close of the period, the Diocese awaited the appearance of the first Church School courses.

To create a spirit of Diocesan unity, the Bishop felt that "The Harrisburg Churchman" should have a wider distribution. The paper had had a checkered career. It was launched by the Special

Convention of 1905 as a missionary enterprise, and its cost was underwritten by 34 men, each of whom agreed to subscribe $10 to cover any deficit provided it did not exceed $25 per subscriber. The first issue appeared in April and was under the editorship of Rev. Robert F. Gibson. At the end of the first year, the deficit was some $542, but the Convention of 1906 decided to continue the venture for another year. Despite the fact that it was a most attractive paper, it was not generally subscribed to by the Diocese so that the deficit was even greater at the end of the second year. Thereupon, Convention determined to suspend publication. The project was revived in the days of Bishop Wyatt-Brown and the paper was ably edited by Canon French. Supported by advertising and by paid subscriptions, it got on fairly well financially. Since it was the only medium by which the Diocese could keep in touch with the people, Bishop Heistand suggested that the paper be sent without cost to every family in the Diocese. Funds from the Field Work budget were allocated to help defray the cost of printing and each recipient was asked to contribute twenty-five cents, and later, fifty cents a year toward its support. While this appeal met a generous response, rising costs made the financial situation precarious. After the retirement of Canon French, the paper had a series of Editors, Rev. Robert C. Batchelder, Rev. Kenneth J. Hafer and Rev. James Stanley. The leaders of the future will face the problem of putting this paper on a sound financial basis and making of it truly a Diocesan organ.

A second charge was made against the field Work budget in 1952 when, at the Bishop's suggestion, the Diocese assumed larger responsibilities for the maintenance of the Shippensburg Episcopal Home for the Aged. When the church at Shippensburg was placed under the care of the Rector at Chambersburg, the large rectory was used as a home for the aged and one of the Chambersburg Rector's responsibilities was to act as Superintendent of the Institution. The home was maintained by endowments, by the entrance fees of the guests and by such desultory contributions as the people of the Diocese were moved to make at Thanksgiving. It was such a small institution that many in the Diocese were hardly aware of its existence. For more than twenty years, Rev. George D. Graeff kept it going despite inadequate support and dwindling endowments.

When Rev. Carlton N. Jones succeeded Mr. Graeff at Chambersburg, he instituted a more aggressive policy toward the home.

Tirelessly going up and down the Diocese, he made the people aware of the home's existence and he urged the Woman's Auxiliaries to take an active interest in supplying the many needs at the home. As a result, donations increased and the Thanksgiving offerings became more substantial. Feeling that the Diocesan family had a definite responsibility to its aged folk, the Executive Council fell in with the Bishop's suggestion to allocate $3,000 a year toward the maintenance of this home, feeling that with increased publicity the institution could be made into a real "home." At this writing, the fiscal policy of the home seems sound, and while the home has a capacity for but a few guests, those who are admitted can look forward to spending their declining years under most pleasant conditions.

The third major increase in the Field Work budget was made to further the work of the Youth Commission. Ever since the young people had been going to the Kiski Conference, the feeling was growing that the Diocese should hold a summer conference within its own bounds. When the Bishop was Chairman of the Youth Commission, he and Miss Helen Owen made arrangements to use the facilities at Central Oak Heights near West Milton. Central Oak Heights had been used for many years by the United Evangelicals as a camp meeting ground and it had been rented to various groups for a similar purpose. The dining lodge and cabins were set in a lovely grove and the place seemed to offer facilities for giving young people a real camping experience. But as a place for study, it left much to be desired. It was most convenient to hold classes outdoors, so when it rained, schedules had to be readjusted. It often happened, that June days were cold so that the days at conference were sometimes quite uncomfortable. Nevertheless a beginning had been made and many still look back upon days at Central Oak Heights with nostalgia.

In 1948, the Bishop came to know the Grier School near Tyrone and its facilities strongly appealed to him as a conference centre. Learning that the owner of the school would be happy to have young people meet there, the conference was transferred there in 1947 and has continued to meet there ever since. Through a program of worship, study and recreation the faith of the young people has been deepened and the bonds of fellowship strengthened. Perhaps no activity has done more for the making of a Diocese consciousness than these gatherings in the summer.

One of the significant outcomes of holding the Youth Conference at Grier has been that the school has become virtually a Diocesan conference center. The clergy used it in 1947 and 1950 for their retreats; the Provincial meeting of the Woman's Auxiliary was held there in 1951 and 1952; the Department of Christian Education used it in 1952 and 1953 for holding Institutes for Church School teachers, and the Brotherhood of St. Andrew held retreats for laymen there in 1953 and 1954. As a result of the contacts with the Bishop and the people of the Diocese, Mr. Thomas G. Grier, owner of the school, became an Episcopalian. Feeling that the school ought to have a definite religious affiliation, he placed it under Church auspices in 1952.

The school which thus became related to the Diocese was established in 1853 by Lemuel G. Grier and was known as the Mountain Female Seminary. In 1915, under the ownership of a son, Alvin R. Grier, the name was changed to the Birmingham School for Girls. When the grandson of the founder became sole owner he felt that the family name should be associated with the school so the present name was adopted. The school is situated in one of the most beautiful spots in central Pennsylvania, high in the Alleghenies with ample facilities for all sorts of outdoor activity. As a college preparatory school it has high academic standing.

Unlike the venture with the Yeates School, the Diocese assumes no financial responsibility for the support of Grier. The Diocese assists in policy making by having the Bishop as a member of the Advisory Board. One of the significant results of the school's relation to the Diocese was the appointment of Rev. Joseph T. Heistand, Rector of Trinity Church, Tyrone, as school Chaplain, the use of the Prayer Book and Hymnal in the Chapel service and the establishment of a class in religion. Diocesan relations have been made closer by the fact that in the summer of 1953 the Chaplain took up residence on the campus.

That the Diocese was moving slowly forward is indicated by the fact that Trinity Church, Renovo, was given its own resident priest in 1944; the work at Lewisburg had progressed so far that St. Andrew's was admitted as an organized mission in 1946, and as a result of a campaign to "Save the Day for Lewisburg" funds were made available to assist the congregation in building a small but attractive church which was opened in 1952. The congregation greatly appreciates this change, since it is no longer necessary to occupy rented quarters in the Congregational Christian Church and the work with the Bucknell students can be more effective.

In 1947, St. Luke's, Mechanicsburg, and Christ Church, Berwick, attained parish status; the old hall in which the congregation of St. Andrew's, York, had been meeting was sold and a new site purchased on which a church building was begun, in the basement of which the congregation had been worshipping since 1949; plans are now under way to complete the building and the church gives promise of becoming a strong parish in that growing section of York. In 1948, Mount Calvary, Camp Hill, became an incorporated parish and in 1954 opened their new church to accommodate their ever growing congregation. In 1950, St. Elizabeth's, Elizabethtown, and St. Michael and All Angels, Middletown, were admitted as organized missions and the Church of the Holy Trinity at Hollidaysburg was made an incorporated parish.

Again and again, the Bishop called the attention of the Executive Council to the unclaimed opportunities at Hanover. At last, in 1951, a congregation was organized there and put in charge of the Vicar of the Church of the Prince of Peace at Gettysburg. Though the congregation worships in inadequate quarters in a house converted to church purpose, All Saints' is an enthusiastic mission which promises to make the Episcopal Church effective in the western part of York County.

On the retirement of Canon E. M. Frear, Rev. John N. Peabody became Vicar at State College. He built well on the foundation that had been laid and when he left the Diocese in 1952, the church was doing an outstanding work with the 600 Episcopal students resident there. For his place, the Bishop secured Rev. Jones B. Shannon, under whose leadership St. Andrew's applied for parish status in 1953 and the money allocated to the work by the various Pennsylvania Dioceses is being used to support an assistant, enabling parish and students to receive a more effective ministry.

On the other hand certain work had to be closel: St. Peter's and St. Barnabas in Altoona; St. Elizabeth, Elizabethtown; Trinity Church, Steelton, and All Saints', Paradise. While recounting setbacks, we must note the fact that in February, 1948, Christ Church, Danville, was completely destroyed by fire. Happily, the congregation set themselves to the task of rebuilding and they will soon have a beautiful church in which to worship.

The years brought sadness to the Diocese in the death of some of its leaders. Frank K. Lukenbach, a member of the Standing Committee for many years and a devoted member of Trinity Church, Tyrone, died in 1948; in 1950, the Diocese mourned the loss of Canon Atkins who for thirty years had been prominent in the counsels of the Diocese and whose happy style could be counted on to convey words of felicitation or condolence. In 1950, the Diocese lost its Chancellor, Mr. Charles L. Miller, and its Retired Bishop Hunter Wyatt-Brown. In August, 1953, the Diocese lost two priests within a week—Rev. John H. Treder, Secretary of the Diocese and a valued member of the Youth Conference staff, and Rev. Francis B. Creamer, Rector of St. Mark's, Lewistown.

Through death and removal, the period brought many changes in leadership to the Diocese and to many of the parishes. Bishop Heistand was succeeded at the Cathedral by Rev. Thomas H. Carson; two years later, he left the Diocese and was succeeded by Rev. Thomas H. Chappell. At Williamsport, Canon Gast was called to Washington and was succeeded by Rev. G. Francis Burrill who remained there till he was elected Suffragan Bishop of Dallas in 1950; Rev. Llewellyn O. Diplock then took his place at Christ Church.

At Trinity, Rev. J. Moulton Thomas resigned in 1944 to take a parish in Wheeling and was followed by Rev. Francis P. Davis who remained till the fall of 1953 when he was called to St. John's Lansdowne; his place was taken by Dr. William B. Williamson, Rector of Grace Church, Honesdale, and Executive Secretary of the Department of Christian Education in the Diocese of Bethlehem.

At Altoona, Rev. John R. Leatherby went to Fort Worth in 1947 and was succeeded by Rev. Donald C. Means, who returned to the Diocese after his military service and a short Rectorship at Beaver Falls in the Diocese of Pittsburgh. Rev. F. William Lickfield left Philipsburg late in 1943 and was succeeded by Rev. Harvey P. Knudsen who had been Vicar at St. Stephen's, Mount Carmel.

Rev. William J. Watts closed a nine-year Rectorship at St. Paul's, Bloomsburg, and was succeeded in the spring of 1953 by Rev.

(130)

Elmer A. Keiser, who had come into the ministry after a long and successful teaching experience in the public schools and had served for a short period as Vicar of St. Luke's, Mount Joy, and St. John's, Marietta.

At St. Matthew's, Sunbury, Rev. George Armstrong was succeeded by Willis R. Doyle, and Rev. W. Josselyn Reed who had been at Brunswick, Maryland, after returning from military service. The period saw the retirement of three veteran priests: Rev. George D. Graeff, Rev. Harry D. Viets and Rev. Charles E. Berghaus. Father Viets' place at Carlisle was taken by Rev. Earl M. Honaman, and when he was called to York, by Rev. John G. Hilton of Mansfield.

These parochial changes were bound to affect the Diocesan organization. On the retirement of Canon Frear, Rev. John R. Leatherbury was made Canon, and on the removal of Archdeacon Lickfield from the Diocese, he was made Archdeacon of Altoona; when he removed to Fort Worth, his place as Archdeacon was taken by Harvey P. Knudsen and his place as Canon by Rev. Donald C. Means. When Archdeacon Hilton was called to Carlisle, Rev. John C. Moore of Coudersport became Archdeacon of Wellsboro.

The Archdeaconry of Harrisburg had two changes of leadership: on the death of Archdeacon McCutcheon, Rev. Earl M. Honaman was elected; on his removal to York, he resigned and his place was taken by Rev. George H. Toadvine. In the Archdeaconry of Williamsport, Archdeacon Schofield was succeeded by Rev. William J. Watts, Rev. Francis P. Davis, and Rev. W. Josselyn Reed. In 1951, Canon Pfafko joined the ranks of the non-parochial clergy and Rev. Carlton N. Jones was appointed to fill his place as Canon of the Cathedral.

The position of Canon Missioner was created in 1949 and Rev. Clifton A. Best, who had done outstanding work in the field of evangelism was appointed to this position by the Bishop. On the death of Charles L. Miller, Mr. Robert Lee Jacobs of Carlisle was elected Chancellor; in 1952, Mr. Lesley McCreath who had served the Diocese efficiently as Secretary-Treasurer for a score of years, felt impelled for reasons of health to resign as Secretary and his place was taken by Rev. John H. Treder; on Mr. Treder's death, the Standing Committee elected Mr. Samuel S. Schmidt to succeed him. In

1953, Mr. McCreath resigned as Treasurer and Mr. Samuel A. Burns was elected to take his place. The Diocese owes a great debt to Mr. McCreath, for it was through his skillful management of Diocesan finances through years of depression that losses on investments were reduced to a minimum.

Various special occasions called the Convention away from the Cathedral. Iin 1944, it met at St. James, Lancaster, in connection with the celebration of the 200th anniversary of the parish. In celebration of this event, the Synod of Washington met there that fall—the second instance of the Synod's meeting in the Diocese, the first being in 1929 when it met at St. Stephen's, Harrisburg. In 1946, Convention met at Trinity, Williamsport, in connection with the celebration of its 80th anniversary. Repairs to the Cathedral took the Convention to St. James, Lancaster, in 1950; two years later, it met in Carlisle to help celebrate the 200th anniversary of that parish, and in 1953 went to St. John's, Lancaster, as a feature of the celebration of their first hundred years as a parish.

Bishop Weyatt-Brown could attend only two of these Conventions. True to the promise made on his retirement, he kept himself in the background and never sought to take the leadership of the Diocese away from Bishop Heistand. He spent his winters at Sewannee where he sometimes attended classes at the University and assisted in the services of the church there; and he spent his summers at Blue Ridge Summit. He usually sent his greetings to the Convention and a place was always reserved for his message on the program of the annual banquet of the Young Peoples' Fellowship. His presence at the Convention of 1951 was an inspiration. He had recovered from a successful operation on his eyes and he seemed happy and full of vigor. No one guessed that before the year was out, he would be taken from the Diocese. A Memorial Service was held for him at the Cathedral on May 1 and the eulogy was delivered by Canon Heber W. Becker.

In 1946 and 1948, the Woman's Auxiliary tried the experiment of holding their Convention at the time of the Diocesan Convention. Since the Bishop was occupied with Convention duties, the women felt that they would do better to meet at a time when he could be with them, so the fall meeting was resumed in 1948. The Diocese received signal honors in the election of Mr. Samuel S. Schmidt to the

National Council and to the Presidency of the Brotherhood of St. Andrew; and in the election of the Bishop to the Presidency of the Province of Washington in 1953. The Korean War called back to the service the Rev. Messrs. Honaman, Means and Reed and added to the list of Chaplains who served from the Diocese the names of Rev. Charles J. James, William H. Weitzel and Albert N. Barrenger. In 1952, the Bishop had the rare privilege of ordaining his son Joseph to the Priesthood and his heart was gladdened to realize that his younger son Hobart was then at Alexandria studying for Holy Orders.

The Diocese closes its first half century at work in every county except Fulton. Fifty priests are in the active ministry; eight are non-parochial and three are serving with the armed forces. It has 74 parishes and missions with a communicant strength of 15,396 and a total membership of 20,509. 4,254 pupils are being trained in its church schools which are staffed by 552 officers and teachers. It operates on a Diocesan budget of $28,965.94 and a Field Work budget of $83,878.00. To celebrate its golden anniversary, arrangements have been made to hold special services of Thanksgiving on May 23, 1954, the Sunday nearest Convention when special prayers and lessons will be read in every church and the offering devoted to the building of St. Andrew's, York. Convention will meet on May 25 at St. James, Lancaster, the birthplace of the Diocese and the speaker at the great service of thanksgiving will be the Presiding Bishop, the Rt. Rev. Henry Knox Sherrill. It is hoped that a service of thanksgiving will be held in each Archdeaconry within thirty days after Convention.

Looking back over the years, one is conscious of opportunities missed, errors of judgment and a lack of devotion. Yet there is much for which to be grateful to God. Three consecrated men of God have furnished capable and self sacrificing leadership; many priests have been faithful shepherds of souls; thousands of devoted laymen have labored to make of their parish churches a Christian fellowship. This is the cloud of witnesses which will surround those who gather at Lancaster for their service of thanksgiving. Thus surrounded, the thanksgiving must be mingled with a sense of grave responsibility as heirs of so goodly a heritage. As they face this re-sponsibility and look forward to the years ahead, they could do no better than to pray as did their Bishop at his Consecration:

"O Master, let me walk with Thee
In lowly paths of service free,
Tell me Thy secret, help me bear
The strain of toil, the fret of care.

Help me the slow of heart to move
By some clear winning word of love,
Teach me the wayward feet to stay
And guide them in the homeward way.

Teach me thy patience still with Thee
In closer, dearer company,
In work that keeps faith sweet and strong
In trust that triumphs over wrong.

In hope that sends a shining ray
Far down the future's broadening way,
In peace which only Thou canst give,
With Thee, O Master, let me live."

BIBLIOGRAPHY

Addison, James Thayer: "The Episcopal Church in the United States" New York, 1951

Darlington, James Henry: "Verses by the Way" New York, 1925

Darlington, James Henry: "Joys of the Christian Ministry" (North American Review), February, 1928

Diocese of Harrisburg: "Journals" 1904-1953

Klein, M. J. and Diller, William F.: "The History of St. James Church" Lancaster, 1944

Miller, Jonathan W.: "History of the Diocese of Central Pennsylvania and the Diocese of Harrisburg" Frackville, 1909

3989